uncharted terriTORI

ALSO BY TORI SPELLING

sTORI telling

Mommywood

uncharted terriTORI

TORI SPELLING

WITH HILARY LIFTIN

G

GALLERY BOOKS
NEW YORK LONDON TORONTO SYDNEY

G

Gallery Books
A Division of Simon & Schuster, Inc.
1230 Avenue of the Americas
New York, NY 10020

First Gallery Books hardcover edition June 2010

GALLERY BOOKS and colophon are trademarks of Simon & Schuster, Inc.

For information about special discounts for bulk purchases, please contact Simon & Schuster Special Sales at 1-866-506-1949 or business@simonandschuster.com.

The Simon & Schuster Speakers Bureau can bring authors to your live event. For more information or to book an event contact the Simon & Schuster Speakers Bureau at 1-866-248-3049 or visit our website at www.simonspeakers.com.

Designed by Jaime Putorti

Manufactured in the United States of America

10 9 8 7 6 5 4 3 2 1

Library of Congress Cataloging-in-Publication Data

Spelling, Tori, 1973–
    Uncharted terriTORI / Tori Spelling.
      p.   cm.
    1. Spelling, Tori, 1973–   2. Actors—United States—Biography.   I. Title.
    PN2287.S664A3   2010
    791.4502'8092—dc22
    [B]   2010015770

ISBN: 978-1-4391-8771-5
ISBN: 978-1-4391-8773-9 (ebook)

To everyone reading this book . . .
Find your hope within and let it inspire you on your journey.
Write your own happy ending!

Contents

uncharted terriTORI

INTRODUCTION:

Welcome to Los Angeles

A few weeks ago my friend Jacob was flying Virgin American from New York to L.A. As the plane began its final descent into LAX, the cute and obviously gay lead flight attendant made an announcement to the cabin. He said, "Welcome to Los Angeles, birthplace and residence of Tori Spelling." When my friend reported this story to me via email, I thought it was hilarious, but I also didn't know exactly what to make of it. I *was* born in L.A. Fact. I still live here. Fact. But on what grounds is that of common interest to an airplane full of diverse travelers? Is it a compliment? Is it a joke? A little of both? Of all the famous people, of all the actors, of all the tabloid darlings, of all the gay icons (if I can call myself that), why me?

But as someone who produces and stars in a show that follows my daily life for the entertainment of millions of people (holy crap!), I can't spend too long on questions like that. After *90210* and so many TV movies, my career had slowed, and recently, in my reality show, it has found new life. The name *Tori Spelling* draws viewers, and it sells magazines, books, a jewelry line, a children's clothing line. And my name also, apparently, occasionally welcomes certain unsuspecting travelers as they arrive in Los Angeles. So it goes. I've come to accept that the small moments of my life, my relationship, my family, my business ventures—usually in edited, broadcast form—are a spectacle. My life is a show. My self is my business. My name is my brand. It's a weird way to live, and maybe I'll never get used to it, but at the same time business is booming.

My life has changed dramatically in the past several years. I married Dean; we moved several times; we had two children; we created a show that has gone into its fifth season on the air. I have love. I have a family. I have a home. I have work. It's all I ever wished for. But trying to be a perfect wife, mother, and mini mogul has its challenges, especially if, like me, you want to be perfect at all of them at the same time.

Turns out I'm officially a workaholic. I think I've always been a bit more driven than anybody realized, myself included. I have ideas. I want to try new things. I see business opportunities. The difference is that before *Tori & Dean* was a success, nobody ever cared what harebrained scheme I was dreaming up. Nobody expected anything of me. Nobody took me seriously. Nobody would have wanted to partner with me. I didn't have the means to make any of it come to pass. Now I have the power. Now there's no excuse not to act on a big idea. Now I can back it up. I have a show. I have two successful lines. I have two bestselling books. I own a well-known brand. (You know, *Tori Spelling*. Who'd a thunk it?)

I was poised to be a workaholic. In the seven years between *90210* and *Tori & Dean,* my acting work came and went. Being an underemployed actor as I was puts the fear in you. *I am nobody. I'll never work again. If I can just get a break I'll make the most of it, I swear.* I developed a strike-while-the-iron's-hot mentality. I don't want to miss a single opportunity.

I'm finally in a position where ideas that I have can actually blossom into businesses. When I shop for new bedding, I can't help thinking, *Maybe I could do a line of Hollywood Regency–inspired shams.* I spend a day doing crafts with the kids and start fantasizing about developing a kids' crafts show or magazine sharing the joys of homemade play dough and pipe cleaner animals. I cook dinner and envision a recipe book with my nanny's special shepherd's pie. I hobble out of an event, barefoot, with four-inch heels in hand, and fantasize about Tori Spelling–branded disposable micro flip-flops. (Somebody please run with that.)

I want to do a show with Dean where we put together dream weddings on a budget: it's on! There's an opportunity for me to do the talk show I've always dreamed of? So what if it's all day, every day, forty-four weeks a year, I want to do it! My agent's worried I'm going to drop dead. *Can we clone me?* I wonder. Nah, the clone wouldn't do it right. Yeah, I got the whole workaholic package, which means I'm so completely incapable of delegating that I couldn't even delegate to my own clone. People talk all the time about leaving work behind at the end of the day, about how important it is to draw a dividing line between your job and your life. But my job is to be Tori Spelling. I can't exactly take a break.

In some ways I feel like I'm turning into my father. Dad was a workaholic. He was productive, work was lucrative, but it never stopped. When I was little I hardly noticed. I thought every father came home long after dinner and baths were over, just in time to kiss his children good night.

Even late in his career, my father never stopped caring about every detail of every show. On weekends he would come home with a briefcase full of scripts. We'd go out to the pool together, I'd click open the briefcase, and we'd sit next to each other reading. He dog-eared the pages where he had notes, just as I now do with scripts. By the time he was finished with a script, every single page would be folded over and every line of the script would be rewritten. When we first started *90210* he even brought home Polaroids of the wardrobe options for Brenda and Brandon. He couldn't delegate either.

Ultimately I feel like my father died because he could no longer work. When he stopped working he went quickly downhill. There was no adjusting to a new focus and pace at that age. He didn't know how to just be.

Twitter—the way I use Twitter, is a perfect example of how it never stops, how I never stop. Sometimes Dean is sleeping next to me in bed while I tweet until one a.m. I tweet what I've prepared for the kids' holiday parties at school. I post what movie I watched that night. I check to see how many followers I have. I check to see how many followers Brooke Burke and Denise Richards have (they're in the big leagues, each with over a million followers). I'm obsessed with how many followers I have and what makes them decide to follow me or to stop following me. If I talk about cute things the kids are doing, my followers drop off. If I retweet news items, people sign on. If I don't tweet for a day, I gain a hundred followers. When I posted that I watched *Paranormal Activity*, I gained fifty-six followers. Why, why, why?

I tell myself I'm doing it for the fans and for my business; I'm building my brand. And I do use Twitter that way. For Little Maven, my kids' clothing line, I went on Twitter to do a model search. People posted photos of their children to Twitter, and I selected models for our look book—a catalogue for retail buyers—and website. My "followers" know that it's me looking at the pictures. I'm the one who's picking their kids. They know that I'm not doing a celebrity endorsement, that I'm actually at the helm of my business. And they also know that I'm the one who's dropping my kids off at school. Because I tweet about it afterwards. It's kind of like I'm stalking myself, but it doesn't feel creepy. It makes me feel connected to people. If I'm going to be a brand, it's nice to feel like people really know me. But I also see how my obsessive twittering can be unhealthy. Nothing is private, nothing is sacred. Dean is asleep next to me, and I should be sleeping too. I'm more stressed than I've ever been in my life.

I haven't found a good balance, and (when he's awake) it doesn't sit well with Dean. A couple of nights ago Dean came into the kitchen and told me he'd run a bubble bath for me—an overt effort to get me to relax. Liam and Stella were running around the kitchen, waiting for me to make them dinner. Dean said, "Don't worry, I've got it." Dean is perfectly capable of making dinner for the kids. Nonetheless, I started pulling out the broccoli, rice, and hot dogs. Just to get him started. Dean stood there staring at me. "What are you doing?" he said, "I just said I've got it." But I couldn't stop myself.

I'm not just controlling when it comes to the kids. I came into the kitchen the other night to find Dean, who is self-sufficient in all things, eating a dinner he'd made for himself. When I saw him sitting there, alone at the table, I felt deflated. "I was going to do that for you," I told him. I wanted to make dinner for him. I wanted us to eat together even if I got home too late. I want to be able to do everything. Then I'm resentful of having to do everything. And that's how it all implodes.

Maybe this is what happens when you finally find success in a career that you love. Maybe it's a side effect of having children. Maybe it's my childhood coming back to haunt me. Whatever it is, it's taking a toll on me, on my health, and on my family. I'm exhausted, if not sick, half the time. The rest of the time my marriage, my family, and my job together are my dream come true. But those two sides of my life—exhausted and elated—are constantly vying for Tori dominance (not quite as critical as world dominance but try telling that to my immune system). The struggle plays out in Malibu and Maui, on a tour of local L.A. hospitals and across the country in an RV. Somehow in realizing my dreams I've lost my ability to just be. My reality is my job, and that means that my work and my life are completely woven together. It all happened so quickly that I haven't begun to establish any boundaries. My life is all out of balance, which has turned out to be a biggie. I got everything I thought I wanted . . . and it practically destroyed me. I need to make a change. I don't know how and when I'll do it, but that search is the challenge and the journey.

Summer at 30,000 Feet

We were still shooting the fourth season of *Tori & Dean* when I noticed a woman who looked familiar on the sidelines of Liam's swim class. Her name was Kathleen, and it turned out that back when I was on *90210* we'd been neighbors. She rented the guesthouse next door to a house in Sunset Plaza that I bought but never lived in. (Let's just say that it's a long story involving evil contractors, a young girl who thought that every home needed a room for the night guardsman, and a lost investment opportunity about which I'm still a little bitter.) Kathleen and I had met once or twice back in the day. She was an actor at the time. She had played a girlfriend of Jerry's on *Seinfeld*—the one who liked to spend most of her time naked.

Kathleen was no longer a young actor renting a small guesthouse. She now lived with her wealthy husband in Brentwood. And I was no longer the rich young star of a hit TV show but a working mom with a big mortgage. In some ways it felt like we'd traded positions. I was drawn to Kathleen immediately. She was warm, energetic, funny—one of those people it was impossible to meet without liking. You don't need time to warm up with Kathleen. You feel as if you know her from the start. She hugs everyone and has an infectious laugh.

As we watched our kids swim, Kathleen and I started up talking about how her family spends the summer in Malibu. Ah, Malibu. Malibu is the dream. The wealthiest of Hollywood's wealthy love to live there or vacation there because it's so close to the metropolis—only thirty minutes from L.A.—yet a stunningly beautiful oceanside paradise. And it's priced accordingly. You've made it if you can spend the summer in Malibu.

I loved the idea of bringing my children to Malibu for the summer. I had fond memories of childhood summers spent in our family's vacation house there. My mother still owned that house, but we wouldn't be spending time there. My mother and I had a (notoriously) troubled relationship. We weren't officially "not speaking," but we also weren't speaking. I told Kathleen that, sadly, Malibu was too rich for our blood. Then Kathleen told me about an apartment available right next to the one her family rented. I was skeptical, but it was actually reasonably priced. A place in Malibu we could kind of almost afford! I texted Dean pronto. We went out to Malibu to see the apartment the next day and signed the lease right away. We were in.

Dean and I decided that as soon as season four finished shooting, we'd take a break. We'd move the family out to Malibu for July and August. It would be a much-needed vacation, but we'd still be close enough for Liam to attend his toddler program through the summer, and for me and Dean to go to the business meetings that were already creeping into our summer schedule.

The first week in Malibu was very promising. When we're filming *Tori & Dean*, there are cameras in our house all day long. We're used to it, and we know the crew so well that they are like family, but (and this is the built-in irony of reality TV) it can never be completely normal to have cameras watching you live your life. Just getting away from home felt like an escape.

We settled into our apartment right away. It was already furnished, but I tried to make it homey. I found a wooden sign that said "Beach House" and propped it on the mantel. I placed big seashells on the coffee table. I put beachy wooden frames with pictures of the kids in the living room.

The initial thrill of Malibu didn't last long for me. I got in the way of my own good time. I was anticipating the three business trips to the East Coast that I had coming up in July. It wasn't a ridiculous commitment, and it was weeks away, but I have a serious, lifelong fear of flying. My full-time dread of those three trips put a stressful shadow over the first half of the summer.

The first trip was to New York to cohost the *Today* show with Kathie Lee. The next week I was going back to New York to do a personal appearance for Q-tips. I was to do a satellite radio tour, then appear in a store window with a makeup artist demonstrating how Q-tips are "the summer beauty rescue of choice." Then, a week after that gig, I had to be in Tampa to promote my jewelry line on HSN. Three trips back to back, week after week after week, but I didn't feel like I could say no to any of them. The

Today show wasn't a paying gig, but it was a huge opportunity and an honor; the Q-tips job was for money; and I'd committed to HSN to make this appearance. The only trip that was truly optional was *Today*, but I dream of hosting a talk show in the future, and having a tape of myself on air with Kathie would be a huge selling point. I might never have this chance again.

If I didn't have Liam and Stella at home, I would have stayed in New York between the first two appearances, hanging out in the hotel for a week just to avoid the extra round-trip on the plane. Three plane trips might not be a big deal to some people, and it might even be exciting to others, but for me it was a nightmare.

My airplane phobia. It just doesn't get better, no matter what I try or how often I fly. My best friend Mehran—he's the one I call my gay husband—says it's actually getting worse. When I moaned about doing East Coast appearances for our jewelry line, I told him I was just too busy with work, but he was on to me. He asked, "What if it were in L.A.? Would you mind doing it then?" I had to admit that flying was the sole reason I wanted to stop. Mehran said, "Your businesses are your livelihood. They include travel. If you keep on this path, you're not going to be able to sustain your businesses."

I saw firsthand how my father's fear of flying limited him. He never ever went on planes. He missed traveling the world, going to family reunions, and—what would have meant the most to him—traveling with his TV shows when they went on location or were promoted to advertisers at the up-fronts in New York every year. I knew I'd taken on his phobia and I certainly didn't want to pass it on to my kids, but I was stuck with it.

Then I happened to be talking to a psychic. (Not for my flying issues but because whenever I hear about a great psychic, I have to go. I explore new psychics the way some people try out new restaurants. If there were a Zagat that reviewed psychics, I'd keep it on my bedside table for handy access.) When this psychic looked at my cards she said, "You are *light* on a flight. People should want to fly with you." I liked the sound of that. I was light. And I was pretty sure she wasn't joining the tabloids in calling me underweight. She meant "light" like "radiant." Or so I told myself. Anyway, after a pause she said, "You know, there's a reason you and your father both have this fear. It is coming from somewhere else, from a past life. You should go to a past life specialist."

Now, I've always known that my father's fear came from the fact that he missed a flight on a plane that then crashed with no survivors. So I never thought our shared phobia's origins were very mysterious. Plane crash. Plane phobia. Scared dad. Scared kid. It didn't take a rocket shrink. Nonetheless, because I love me some other world specialists, I was immediately curious about my past lives. Maybe I was born into wealth as punishment for my behavior as an Egyptian pharaoh. Maybe I loved pugs because I'd been one. Everything would make sense if I were a gay man in one or more past lives. I said, "Sign me up!"

Disappointingly, the past life lady didn't uncover any past life as a bomber pilot or Amelia Earhart as the root of my airplane phobia. Instead she just said, "Oh, this is because of your dad." Yeah, tell me something I don't know. Instead of going into my past lives, she wanted to cure my phobia through hypnosis. And as fate would have it, this was one of her specialties. I didn't love the idea of being hypnotized. I like to be in control. But this wasn't a creepy "look into my eyes," pocket watch trance. She just put on a headset and started talking on a microphone, leading me on an overamplified phobia-free journey through the process of flying.

The guided meditation went something like, "You're boarding the plane. You're relaxed. You're sitting in your seat. Everything's fine. We're taking off. It's all good. The kid in the seat behind you is kicking your seat. No problem. The kid in the seat behind you is about to projectile vomit. No worries."

At the end of our session, the past life specialist gave me a tape recording of the guided meditation. She told me I should listen to it as I was getting on the plane. And you know, I suspect that if I listened to that tape, it really might help. But the truth is that I didn't listen to it. Not once. I can't really explain why I failed to help myself. How hard could it be to listen to a simple tape before my next flight? But isn't it part of human nature to be stuck in your own bad ways? I'd done my time in therapy, and now, I'll admit it, I was in the market for a magic cure. And besides, listening to the tape was too complicated. Hasn't anyone told past life specialists that nobody has cassette players anymore? Where was my hypnosis podcast? That would be the sole criticism I had to make in my Zagat review of the past life specialist. She gave "inspired" guided meditation but she had "outdated technology."

The time came for the first trip of the summer. I made it to New York, of course, as I always did, with my typical cocktail of anxiety, tears, and abject terror. On the *Today* show I joined Kathie

Lee for the fourth hour, during which they do lifestyle segments on scintillating topics such as whether skinny jeans are bad for your health (turns out they are bad for your vag) and good pickup lines (I told Kathie Lee if she were a fart she would've blown me away. Dean has nothing to worry about: my pickup lines couldn't land me a date on an Alaskan fishing boat).

I was to cohost with Kathie Lee for three days. The first day went smoothly, but we didn't have quite the rapport we wanted. While Kathie Lee ribbed me freely, I wasn't entirely comfortable busting her balls. It seemed disrespectful.

After we finished the first day Kathie Lee turned to me and asked, "What are you doing for the rest of the day? What are you doing for lunch?"

I said, "I'm here with my friend Dana. I was just going to go back to the hotel and brush up on summer barbecue tips for tomorrow."

Kathie Lee said, "I know what you're doing. You're coming to my house in Connecticut. My driver will take us and then he'll bring you and Dana back." I was taken off guard. I'm from L.A. To me Connecticut is just another tiny rectangle on the right-hand side of a United States map puzzle. Were we really going to another state? For lunch? But I had faith in Kathie Lee. We accepted the invitation with pleasure.

The driver took the three of us an hour and a half outside the city to Kathie Lee's beautiful lakeside home in Connecticut. We came up the cobblestone driveway, and suddenly, it was the most amazing thing, it was as if we were in the south of France. It was all leafy and quiet and bucolic.

Inside the house, Kathie Lee asked, "Would you like wine? White wine?" It hadn't occurred to us, but yes, that sounded lovely. She disappeared and returned in a flash with three glasses of perfectly chilled white wine. Then she said, "I'm going to take you outside. Do you have sunglasses?" Well, actually we'd forgotten them . . . so Kathie Lee disappeared again and emerged with sunglasses for us. She was a real hostess, guiding us pleasantly through the visit, anticipating our every desire in the nicest way.

She led us in our borrowed sunglasses out onto an upper patio. The house must have been on a peninsula: every angle seemed to offer a new idyllic vista. This patio overlooked sprawling lawns and a marina. Kathie Lee said, "This was Kevin Costner's favorite spot." We sipped our wine and chatted. Then, after what seemed like the exact right amount of time for patio wine sipping, Kathie Lee said, "Ready to move on?"

She led us down a few steps to another stone balcony with a different but equally spectacular view. Here, amazingly, was a table already perfectly set for us with chicken paillard over arugula salad and a wine bucket awaiting the great bottle of wine we'd started, but not a soul in sight. It was magical. I could get used to this.

As we ate the delicious lunch, Kathie Lee asked me about making *Tori & Dean* and what it's like having cameras follow us all day and night. She didn't know how I could do it. But she'd been on *Live with Regis and Kathie Lee* for fifteen years! She knew better than I what it was like to be in a constant spotlight. Then she explained that at a certain point she realized she had to get away from it all. She wanted her kids to have a normal life. So she left the show, moved her family to the country, and built a new life.

Even years later, when the opportunity to cohost the *Today* show came along, Kathie Lee wasn't sure she would return to the spotlight. But she had an amazing lunch with future cohost Hoda Kotb, was sold on the job, and found a way to make it work. Having this place, outside the city, where she could escape the hustle-bustle of Manhattan and television, where her family already had a real life, was the only way she could do it—on her own terms. It was a real moment for me—hearing how she had gone through a struggle that I was just beginning to recognize, and hearing how she had resolved it. Our polished hostess was engaged, honest, and in the moment. And then, when the time was right, she moved us right along to dessert. Here was a woman who had it all figured out. She was enjoying herself, but she was also making conscious decisions about how to spend her time.

After we all enjoyed sorbet-filled coconuts (Kathie Lee shared a hostess secret: they were from Costco), she said, "You girls ready? My driver is waiting." She ushered us to the car and we were spirited back to the city. It was a perfectly directed visit, so elegantly choreographed. She was extraordinarily polite and charming, the best hostess ever. I was fascinated and impressed. She was right: the home and life she made worked for her. That place did feel like a sanctuary from the other life she led in New York. You could sit there and never have a care in the world.

My life was *sooo* complicated. Later, from the fluffy St. Regis bed, I called Dean back in Malibu and said, "Kathie Lee has it all figured out. *This* is what we need to do . . ."

I totally needed that lunch to feel comfortable on the air with Kathie Lee. Now we were like girlfriends. We'd laughed together; we'd cried together; we'd joked together. Those two hours had bonded us, and the next morning back on the *Today* show, our rapport was awesome. I even felt comfortable enough to give her a nickname: I called her KL from then on.

When my *Today* show gig was over, I flew home from New York and arrived back in Malibu at 8:30 at night. I spent some time with Liam and Dean (Stella was already asleep), then went upstairs and crawled into bed. All that day Dean and I had been texting back and forth. *I miss you so much. I can't wait to see you.* After Liam fell asleep, Dean joined me in bed. We cuddled, and he asked if I wanted to have sex. I was not in the mood. I was more than not in the mood. I had cohosted the *Today* show for three days in a row, and whenever I wasn't in the studio I was doing my homework for the next day's show or doing press surrounding my appearance. Flying home—I don't know how to describe what I go through when I fly—the heart palpitations, the hyperventilating, the panic, the anxiety, the tears. It is physically exhausting. Instead of being relieved that the trip was over, I was already stressing about the next flight for Q-tips (though I was excited to say that they were the summer beauty rescue of choice).

Ordinarily if I'm not in the mood I'll hesitate and coyly say, "I don't know, babe . . ." and the idea trails away. But this time I was actually angry. I said, "Do you know how hard I've been working? I'm so tired. How about tomorrow?" He rolled over and said, "Okay."

Yeah, well. As they say (or should say if they don't), it even rains in Malibu, and the next morning was cloudy in our apartment. When I asked Dean what was wrong, he said, "This is the beginning of the end." That's Dean's code for "Our sex life is over. You're turning into Mary Jo. The marriage is doomed."

I said, "I'm not your ex-wife. I'm genuinely tired. I'm exhausted." I didn't tell him that I was kind of upset that he hadn't read my mind and known not to put the moves on me.

Dean said, "But we haven't seen each other. When we first met you'd work ten-hour days filming and still want to have sex. It's just changed." He had a point. I did not have the exact same sex drive as I had when swept up in a brand-new relationship with no children clamoring for my attention. Was this breaking news? Attention, men of the world: having children, caring for children, loving children affects the sex drives of all women. Your hot little girlfriend will change when she's a mother. You will be frustrated and feel rejected. She will be annoyed and feel misunderstood. The two of you will enter an indefinite period wherein the number of times per week you want to have sex is widely disparate. You will work on it. You will both have to compromise. This is a scientific, evolutionary reality. Don't ask me for the studies to support it. Just trust me. The sooner you accept this, the better.

Of course I didn't lecture Dean about sexual trends in parents of small children. I just reminded him, "I used to stay up late because I could sleep in. Now I don't have that option. Last night I needed to sleep."

"You're more in love with the bed," he said grumpily, and that was the end of it, but not really.

Like it or not, it was to be the summer of flying, but at least I could count on August. After the last of my trips, to HSN, I'd be able to relax in Malibu for a few weekends.

Not so fast. Upon my return from HSN, I got an envelope I'd seen a few too many times in the past. I'd been called for jury duty. Uh-oh. This was it. My time had come. I'd postponed jury duty so many times—for work, for nursing babies, for more work, for more babies—that now if I didn't step up and do my civic duty I was at risk of being in contempt of court. I couldn't exactly call in and say, "Hello? I'm, like, vacationing in Malibu. It's been a tough summer because I had to cohost with Kathie Lee. You know how it is. But I have this neighbor in Malibu, Kathleen? She's been relaxing all summer. Perhaps she could fill in for me?" No, I couldn't say that.

So I dutifully called in to the jury line all week long, and then, on Thursday, just when I was starting to think I was off the hook, I was told to report to the courthouse the next morning at seven a.m.

I crawled out of bed at the crack of dawn to make the long commute from Malibu to downtown L.A. Dean hoisted himself up on his elbows and smiled. "Don't worry," he said. "They're not going to pick you. How random and weird would that be? Having a celebrity on a jury makes no sense. Imagine if they have a trial; they're not going to pick Harrison Ford. He's going to sway all the jurors."

"Do I look like Harrison Ford to you?" Dean threw a pillow at me.

"You know what I mean," he said.

I made the long drive downtown, parked in the Disney Music Hall, and entered the courthouse. As I got into line everyone was staring at me, as if they couldn't figure out why I was there. Had I been arrested for shoplifting? Was I filing divorce papers? Was being too thin finally declared a crime? Sorry, guys, no juicy scandal. Just regular old jury duty like the rest of you.

I overheard the woman in front of me saying that she expected to be called soon because she was in group number two. I looked down at my jury notice. I was in group eighty-four. It was like winning the lottery—in an alternate universe where you can get a bad ticket that strips life of all hope and joy.

At long last I was admitted to a large room full of fellow potential jurors. There was nothing to do but wait. As I waited I noticed that the wall was elegantly decorated with plaques commemorating celebrities who had served as jurors in the past. Only in L.A. are the courtroom walls made into another stop on the Hollywood Hall of Fame Tour. There was Camryn Manheim, Ed Asner, Weird Al, and Edward James Olmos. And there, for Dean's and my edification, was Harrison Ford himself. So much for Dean's theory. If Harrison Ford could be picked for a jury, then I definitely could be picked for a jury.

Then it started to dawn on me how bad that would actually be. What if I got put on a trial? In two weeks, at the beginning of September, we were supposed to start filming season five! People were depending on me! I was panicking. I looked desperately around the room. It was filling up with all sorts of people. Everyone was somber and officious. There was no way out. I was doomed.

Then I saw it. A line of computers on the wall labeled "For Juror Access." I strolled over and glanced at the rules. Maybe this was my salvation. Was it possible that I could actually shop online while fulfilling my civic duty? A huge sign above the computers said something about not looking at porn. Did fashion count as porn? Because I happened to know that there was a sale launching at eleven a.m. on gilt.com, a members-only discount shopping website where I was a regular. If I managed to score some Moschino Cheap and Chic, this would all be worth it. Looking over my shoulder so as not to be busted for my dirty little fashion habit, I logged on. Access accepted! I was in. Jury duty be damned, Moschino was mine!

I did some damage on the website, and all the while the clerk was calling out numbers, getting closer to mine. I was nervous about checking in with the clerk. I'm always nervous in public because I feel like people are thinking, "Oh, *her*," and looking to find fault with me. So I use a little voice, and I try to be really respectful and overly nice, apologizing constantly. When she finally called my number, I scurried up to the desk and whispered a timid hi to the clerk. She glanced up at me, gave me a knowing smile, and said, "I have to announce everyone's name, but don't worry. I'll keep it low-profile. I'm going to change your name to Victoria Spellman." I nervously thanked her.

As I hurried back to my seat I had instant regrets. I was already wishing I'd told her to just use my real name. Victoria Spellman? Would people think that my legal name was Victoria Spellman and that Tori Spelling was my stage name? Would they think I was trying to hide or get special treatment? I didn't want them to think that! Shoot, should I turn around and tell the clerk not to do it? But she was already on to the next group. If I turned around, everyone would look at me and wonder what diva celebrity request I was making. I didn't want to make a scene. If I turned around now, it would just make me stand out, which was exactly what I was trying to avoid. It was hopeless. I didn't say anything, of course. I just slumped down in my seat, defeated.

Soon the clerk called "Group one!" She read all the names in that group, waiting for each person to say, "Here." If someone didn't speak up quickly or loudly enough, she called the name again. My heart was pounding. Bad enough she was going to say my fake name once; I had to be sure there was no need for her to say it twice. Under my breath, I practiced saying "here" to make sure she heard me the first time.

The first group came and went. She called the second group. Wow, they really were going by number. Wow, my ticket really did say group eighty-four. I had some time. I decided that I knew my one-word line well enough and could stop practicing my delivery of "here." I settled in for the long wait.

The third group was called. I checked my BlackBerry. No cell service. No texting. No twittering. The fourth group was called. It seemed utterly impossible that they would ever get to eighty-four. I was doomed to spend the rest of my life trapped in the bureaucracy of this courthouse. We broke for lunch and I went to the cafeteria to get a cheeseburger. People started asking to take pictures, so as my burger cooled to room temperature I did a makeup-free photo session. Then I wolfed down my burger to hurry back and wait several more hours.

Finally, at four p.m., the clerk called, "Victoria Spellman." I shouted, "Here!" at perfect volume. And they say I can't act.

My group of about six people lined up. They handed us IDs with our juror numbers. I was no longer Victoria Spellman. Now I was juror number sixty-nine. Sixty-nine! Oh, come on! I looked up at the official faces around me. Was someone trying to be funny? Apparently not.

I went into the mini courtroom for my case. The plaintiff, defendant, and lawyers were all in suits, lined up in front of the judge. Ah, the memories. I hadn't been in court since the movie *Mind over Murder*, where I played a clairvoyant ADA. It was just like old times, except this go-round I couldn't read people's minds, and I had no adorable Dean McDermott to costar with me.

We stood lined up in the courtroom as they told us about our case. Some guy had taken ideas from one electronics company to another after he'd been fired. As the clerk described the case, the lawyers kept looking at us to see our reactions. I immediately decided to play dumb blonde. Every time the clerk used a technical word, I made sure to look super confused. *Data?* What's *data?* My consolation if they put me on the jury was that I'd successfully purchased a Moschino blazer at a radical discount that would set the perfect serious but stylish tone if I had to go to trial.

Then the clerk dropped a major bomb. She told us that this case was going to last at least three weeks. *Three weeks!* I gasped.

They had told us that most cases only lasted a week. That was my entire vacation. We were supposed to start season five in two weeks. And what if the case ran over, which it would, I just knew it. My dumb blonde act was out the window. Now I was a visibly panicked control-freak workaholic executive producer realizing that if I was on this jury our entire season was going to be delayed, creating a massively expensive production disaster.

The clerk went on. If for some reason we felt we could not miss work for three or more weeks, we would have to show monetary hardship. She said, "We've cracked down on this. You have to really be able to prove that it'll be costing you your income. Like you'd lose your house. Any questions?" She looked directly at me as if to say, "Don't think you can get out of this just because you're a spoiled, rich celebrity." A few people raised their hands. Maybe one of them would have exactly the same issue and I wouldn't have to ask my question. I looked around. I didn't recognize any other reality TV star/producers who were worried about delaying season five. Reluctantly, I half raised my hand. "Yes, juror sixty-nine?"

I suppressed the desire to ask to have my number changed and said, "What if my employment directly affects other people?" With a steely gaze, she handed me a form and said, "You have five minutes to fill this out." She pointed me toward the hall.

I hurried outside. I had five minutes. Should I call Oxygen, our network? My producers? My lawyer? If I was gone we wouldn't make our air date. This wasn't about me. All the crew had been hired; they'd passed up other jobs. Many, many people would lose significant income if I wasn't there to launch the show. Time was running out. I scribbled that out as best I could explain it and submitted it back in the room.

A few minutes later someone came out and said, "Juror sixty-nine and juror sixty-seven, please come with me." A man in jeans and a T-shirt and I were led into a side chamber, where we were told, "You're officially excused." When we went back to the courtroom the other jurors looked at us enviously. They glanced past me, assuming I had undoubtedly played some holier-than-thou celebrity card, but they turned to the other guy and said, "What did you write?"

I left the room maintaining a look of quiet respect for my fellow jurors, the judge, the great American judiciary, but the minute I got into the hall I did an air pump. Sorry, Camryn Manheim, Ed Asner, Weird Al, and Edward James Olmos. Sorry, Harrison Ford. This dumb blonde was off the hook. I had no more plane flights scheduled. I was free from jury duty. Malibu, here I come!

Malibu Tori

It was August. I still had three weekends left to enjoy Malibu. During the week Dean and I had meetings—about shows, websites, movies; the meetings always multiplied so fast that we had to put "free time" on the calendar if we wanted to make sure we had any. So we made sure to keep the weekends clear. Early in the summer I'd bought an inflatable pool for the kids at the drugstore down the street. One day when Dean was away racing his motorcycle, Mehran and I had blown it up. It took forever—turns out a lot of air goes into those things!—but finally we had a respectable (though not fully inflated) pool and the kids had a little dip. The next weekend I came out to the beach to find that Kathleen had put out an inflatable pool the size of a living room. An air hose was attached with an automatic pump. A pump! It hadn't even occurred to me. Of course we upgraded to using Kathleen's fancy inflatable pool for the rest of the summer.

We went biking with the kids (and the ten paparazzi who always accompanied us) to a cute shake shop called the Vitamin Barn, where Stella was obsessed with reorganizing the vitamin bottles on the shelves. She's a neat freak. We had playdates with my best friends Jenny and Sara and their kids, playing on the beach while Dean went paddleboarding. Dean grooved on Malibu's work-to-live culture. Everyone was relaxed, tanned, and beautiful in a bohemian-surfer-meets-billionaire-mogul way. There was only one major obstacle to our good time: Malibu was completely infested with paparazzi.

Over time as a celebrity you start to recognize the paparazzi who follow you. You come to know who's the pushiest, who covers what part of town, and who's going to be polite enough to give the kids space. The L.A. paparazzi are nice, in a fake kind of way. They'll say, "Just one more picture, then I'll leave, I promise." It's never just one more picture, of course, but at least they sound sensitive to the effect they're having on our lives. In New York the paparazzi are straight-out aggressive and relentless. There's no pretense of civility: they just attack. Come to think of it, the paparazzi on both coasts are pretty true to the caricatures of their cities.

Malibu had its own paparazzi culture. There was a whole new group of photographers. Dean and I were amused by the culture difference: the Malibu paparazzi were laid-back surfer guys with an odd preference for hiding behind trees or walls. In L.A. and New York they never hide. But in Malibu they'd peer out sneakily with just a camera lens. Then one would jump out and start shooting face-to-face. As soon as the first photographer revealed himself, they'd all flood in to score their shots. It was a funny ritual.

In our regular life, the paparazzi problem is for the most part contained and manageable. During the day, I avoid Robertson Boulevard, where paparazzi lurk to photograph boutique shoppers. I shop at not-as-trendy boutiques and eat at small restaurants. Night isn't ever a problem. For me, anyway. I guess they disperse to chase down the underwear-free set as they hit the clubs.

But in Malibu there's only one marketplace to shop. There's only a limited choice of restaurants. And the paparazzi didn't seem to be spending as much time surfing as it looked like they did. Every single time we went out, a pack of ten paparazzi followed us. Knowing that the paparazzi were everywhere, I should have assumed I was being photographed on the beach. With no makeup. While talking or eating. Instead, more than once, I'd find out the next day when there were seventeen pictures of me on some website, all of them with my mouth open in one of those horrid in-the-middle-of-animated-conversation shots. Why do pictures of people talking look so unflattering? And why were those the ones they chose to post of me? I've seen millions of cute shots of celebs on the beach, but not me. I know I shouldn't care, but I do. I'm compulsively compelled to look at every unflattering shot on my BlackBerry, thinking, *This is forever available to anyone who wants to write a mean article about me.*

The most dramatic moment came when we went to Taverna Tony, a lively Greek restaurant in the Malibu Country Mart. Halfway through dinner Stella had gotten cranky so Dean had already taken her home. Liam and I finished our meal, and as we left the restaurant we were hit with a barrage of flashes. At home when the paparazzi follow us at night, it's because we're at an event, so Liam and Stella aren't with us. They haven't been exposed to bright nighttime flashbulbs. Even at the party for my book *Mommywood*, we knew what to expect, so we had Liam in sunglasses. This time, when the photographers burst out and began shooting right up in Liam's face, he started screaming and crying, "Ow, my eyes! You hurting my eyes!"

I said, "Buddy, you're okay." Then, holding my hand up to the paparazzi, I said, "Please, please."

Liam said, "I can't see. Ow!" He was rubbing his eyes. My heart fell. The photographers didn't give a shit. They wouldn't stop. We pushed through to get to our car.

When I tweeted about the assault, one of my followers tweeted back saying, "You'll do a reality show, but you freak out about paparazzi?" Fair enough question, even if it was rhetorical, but all I can say is that it's different. I'm a parent, and I have a job on a reality show. My children are involved, and I watch how it affects them and have control over it if it ever becomes a problem. The kids are perfectly comfortable with our cameras. There are no lights that flash in their eyes, but it's more than that. When I came into the living room the other day and the two *Tori & Dean* camera guys, Mario and Ryan, were already here, Mario was throwing Liam up in the air and Liam was saying, "Again, again!" Ryan was pushing a stroller with a Cabbage Patch doll inside while Stella ran next to him saying, "Go! Go!" If Liam started to cry, Mario would put the camera down and comfort him. Liam says that Mario—he calls him Mo—is his best friend. When people speculate that being on a reality show is bad for our kids, what they don't get is that these guys are like uncles. They're almost as close to Liam and Stella as our friends the "Guncles," Bill and Scout.

People don't know what happens behind the scenes of our "behind the scenes" show, which allows them to judge, but this is what really goes on. Filming our show is not a cold business where everyone is disconnected. If it were—and I guess it could have turned out that way—I don't think I could stand it. Especially if Mario weren't there. Mario has been with us from the start. He's known me since I was pregnant with Liam, so Liam doesn't know life without him. Making the show is an intimate experience. We eat lunch and dinner together. When we travel, after we put the cameras away, we call one another's rooms and all meet up for a drink at the bar. It's not a formal working relationship. Our cameramen are like family members.

The paparazzi are a completely different story. They are strangers to Liam, and they don't care about him. If Liam were to cry in front of a paparazzo, the guy would never stoop down to comfort him the way Mario would. The paparazzo would just keep at it. Because a shot of me trying to calm an upset child is probably something he can sell to a tabloid, which will then use it to show that I'm "just like you" or that I'm a terrible parent, depending on what story they're running about me that week. So while the reality cameras and the paparazzi cameras may look the same from the outside, they're just not.

Liam is also starting to notice when fans ask to take a picture with me. He says, "No pictures. No pictures of Mommy." That's a harder one. I want to have a relationship with my fans, and Liam's not afraid, he just doesn't want someone monopolizing my time. But unlike the mad rush of paparazzi, fans are polite and more human, and Liam can see that. There is room for us to talk about the situation and for me to help him through it.

There was one paparazzo in Malibu who stood out from the rest. He was a guy in his twenties, cute, with rumpled dark blond hair. He was shooting video for TMZ. He had a dry sense of humor and impeccable timing. Instead of asking the same old stupid questions—"Hey, Tori, how's your mom? How much do you weigh? Are you and Dean fighting? You gonna get pregnant again? Are you going back to *90210*?"—he asked questions that, for whatever reason, happened to be relevant. When he asked if Dean was going to start surfing, the two of them got into a conversation about the waves. After that, whenever we saw him we referred to him as "our friend." Dean would say, "We've got paparazzi to the left. Our friend's here."

One day when I was on my way to Ralph's, the supermarket, I realized that a paparazzo was following me. When I registered the car shadowing my every move, I felt instant road rage. I wasn't in the mood. I just wanted to buy dinner for my family in peace, for once. I parked the car and saw him pull in behind me. I sat in the driver's seat, trying to decide what to do. Dean and the kids were back at home, waiting for me to bring home dinner. We needed food, but I didn't want to give him the shot. I knew it would be silly to let him affect what or how my family got their dinner, but I was angry.

Then Brooke Burke's husband, David Charvet, came out of the market carrying his daughter. For a moment I couldn't help wishing that the paparazzo would shift his attention to him. No such luck.

I pulled out of the parking lot, empty-handed and pissed. I sped down the street and veered into another market, a smaller, organic store called PC Greens. It was getting dark out, so I couldn't tell for sure, but I thought I'd lost the paparazzo. Then, on my way out of the store, I saw the same car. He *had* followed me here. But then who should pop out of the car but our friend, the TMZ guy. When he saw my face he said, "What's wrong, Tori? You don't want to talk today?"

I said, "Not really." He asked why. I couldn't explain all of it, how sometimes I just couldn't take it anymore, so I just said, "I don't have makeup on."

He said, "Oh please. You couldn't look bad if you tried." Aw. I wasn't being chased by some faceless hound. This one was human.

Another time when we were chatting on camera with our friend, he asked, "How's the mother-daughter feud?" My mother had just written "An Open Letter to Middle-aged Reality Stars (like my daughter)" and sent it to TMZ. Our friend didn't usually bug me with the worst, most gossipy questions, but I let it slide. I was holding Stella, so I turned to her and said, "Stella, are we feuding? When did that happen?" Our friend laughed and left it alone, but the next day when we had just gotten in our car at the Malibu Country Mart parking lot, there was a knock at my window. It was our friend again. He indicated that he didn't have his camera with him and asked me to roll down the window, and when I did he said, "I'm sorry about yesterday." I knew he was talking about the mother-daughter comment. He went on,

"I hope I didn't offend you. You guys have been really cool, but I have a job to do, and they want me to ask those questions."

I said, "You have to do your job. I respect that."

He said, "Cool, see you later," and left. He didn't ask for anything or shoot any footage. He'd come over solely to apologize.

Dean and I were impressed and fascinated. Was there any way to do that job without being a jerk? He was trying.

My final run-in with our paparazzo friend came at the end of the summer. We were having a small gathering at the apartment to celebrate Mehran's birthday. I went out to pick up all Mehran's favorite things: some rosé champagne, caviar, cornichons, a cake, and three flower arrangements. When I parked outside our apartment, a few paparazzi cars were stationed in front, as usual. I saw one of them getting out of his car. I looked over and it was our friend. He said, "Can you help me out with something? I'm supposed to get footage of celebrities giving their favorite hangover cures." Dean wasn't home; he had gone to drop Jack off. I had a carload of party supplies. So I said, "Will you help me carry this stuff in? Fair trade?"

He said, "Sure!"

So he raised his camera and said, "Hey Tori, what's your cure for a hangover?"

I said, "Oh, I'm a mom. I don't know the last time I was hung over, but the best cure is sex." As soon as it came out of my mouth I thought, *Me and my big mouth. That's definitely going to get me in trouble. I don't know how exactly, but it will.*

Satisfied, our friend put the camera down, helped me carry all the groceries and flowers into the apartment, and stayed to set up a little. It felt so strange to have a paparazzo—someone I'm always hiding from, keeping at bay—in my own home. The place was a total mess. That's right, Harvey Levin, I'm a complete slob. You heard it here first. And who knew what incriminating personal items inquiring eyes might find—Gas-X? Nail fungus cream? Odor-Eaters? Superabsorbency pads?

Bringing a paparazzo into our place ran completely against everything I usually do. But somehow I knew that this one was human. He could have taken pictures or called in some tidbit about how we live, but he didn't, and I knew he wouldn't.

I like to imagine that all the paparazzi are a little like our friend. We liked his personality, but even if they aren't all so funny and charming, they all have jobs to do. They all have bosses pressuring them to ask certain questions. They all have lives to live, families to feed. I fantasized about putting together a "They're just like us" photo essay showing the relatable lives of tabloid photographers as they pumped gas and bought coffee. With maybe just one or two unflattering shots taken while they were talking or eating French fries. If somehow the humanity shone through, maybe we could better coexist. Our friend found the balance between doing his job and respecting his fellow humans. And it made him better at his job. I think that's true no matter who you are or what your job is: if you're mindful of the effect you're having on others, you create a better world.

Now that I finally had time to spend in Malibu, I found myself fascinated with my Malibu neighbor Kathleen. Liam and her son

Luke would play together, and Kathleen and I would chat. I liked her; she was earthy and funny and full of energy. She picked up new hobbies easily. The first time we came out to the beach she said, "Look, I just put up these pictures." She'd taken up photography. She started playing the guitar while we were there. She took walks on the beach in a caftan at sunset.

When I was in New York championing Q-tips as the summer beauty rescue of choice (sorry, I just love saying that), Kathleen had emailed me to ask if Liam wanted to have a playdate with Luke. I wrote back that I was in New York. She said, "Oh, what have you been doing?" When I told her, she said, "Oh, that's amazing. I just finished my coffee and am wondering if I should walk on the beach or go paddleboarding."

Now, seeing how anxious I was even when we were walking on the beach, Kathleen said to me, "You're stressed out because you work so hard. I remember what that was like. There was a time when I couldn't not work. Now I'm the total opposite. I don't want to do anything. I did nothing today." I knew it wasn't true; she was always busy. Maybe all she did some days was drive into town, get her hair done, meet her trainer, and play with her son, but she was busy living the life that she chose. Being a mother. Being happy. She looked really happy. And much as I liked her, I was seething with envy.

While Kathleen was busy planning her Christmas cards (in August!), I was constantly jockeying for more time with my children. I could barely remember the first year of Stella's life. How did she get so old so fast? Sometimes it felt like her childhood was flying by. Was this that clichéd feeling of "they grow up so fast," or was I actually missing out on being a mother? It was a sensitive point for me. Although working on *90210* was an amazing experience that I wouldn't trade for anything, I've never gotten over the feeling that it meant I missed my twenties. I never went to college. I always want to make sure that I'm deliberate about deciding how to spend my time and at what cost.

Dean doesn't seem to have the same inner conflict about how he spends his time. When Dean has free time, he spends some of it with the kids and some of it doing other stuff, whereas I feed all my free time directly to Stella and Liam's hungry mouths. Maybe men don't have the same connection to the kids or the same sense of responsibility or, most likely, the same unrelenting guilt.

That summer, when Dean and I talked about my working mom issues, I threatened to quit everything. I could just stop. Stay home with the kids. Do crafts and help out at their school. Take on just enough work to get by. We could sell our house and move to the beach. We could downscale our lives: work less, spend less, live more. I said, "Maybe I shouldn't go on like this. Maybe I don't want to work so hard. Maybe I don't need this life anymore."

Dean answered, "I don't need to live this way. I didn't grow up like this. We have way too much."

Sometimes I agreed. Dean could list many things he liked about our summer, but what I loved most were the times when we escaped it all, even the beauty of Malibu. I was happiest when the four of us were ensconced in that two-bedroom apartment. It was cozy. We were all on top of each other. We didn't need a baby monitor. Liam's crib was in our room next to the bed. Stella was right in the other bedroom because she can't sleep when I'm in the room. While we were in Malibu I regretted buying our house. It was too big. I could see being so happy in that apartment. I've always liked cozy spots. I never wanted a big house like those I grew up in. Now all our money was in a big house where, not for the first time, I felt lost and out of place. Was this why I was working so hard? So we could afford to live in a house that I'd never wanted?

Again, Dean was right there with me. He said, "Let's do it. Let's sell our house and rent this apartment." We both felt that our lives were sprawling out of control. We were too busy. Our house was too big. Our lives were too complicated. I, in particular, was at once too worked up and too exhausted to even enjoy our Malibu reprieve. Maybe what we needed wasn't a summer in Malibu. Maybe we needed a different life.

We considered it. I tried to imagine life without work. That line of thought always brought me back to the age of twenty-six. *90210* had just ended. I spent most of my time home, alone, brainstorming. Maybe I got more spontaneous pedicures than I do now, but I didn't enjoy the freedom because I was so worried about never working again. I still had some income from the show, and I didn't have to worry about supporting anyone but myself. But what I did worry about was securing everything that I have now. A happy family, a place for us to live, an income to support us. It's impossible for me to long for that time when this is what I wanted.

Dean and I talked about these things, but the fact was that I was still the same person who made those choices in the first place. I couldn't really imagine living any other way. No amount of work, stress, missing the kids, or envying Kathleen was going to change me. I don't think Dean meant to call my bluff, but as soon as he signed on to a simpler life, I saw that my threats were a worthless exercise in self-pity.

Then I thought about the kids' toys. And my closet. All those shoes. All those beautiful designer shoes. They needed a proper home.

In the end, Malibu didn't add up to a vacation for me. But let's not blame Malibu. Malibu held up its end of the bargain (if *Malibu* and *bargain* can be used in the same sentence). It's not Malibu's fault that I'm afraid of flying and incapable of unwinding. It's not Malibu's fault that I got called for jury duty. It's not Malibu's fault that even when I did have time there, I tried to relax, mostly failed, and then it was over and we came back home. A week later I loved our house again. I loved my work. I never stopped loving my family. But I still yearned for a real vacation.

The Haunting in Maui

I have to rewind a little. Malibu wasn't the first time that summer I failed to properly relax in an oceanside paradise. Before we booked our Malibu rental in Kathleen's building, we'd already planned a trip to Maui for the beginning of the summer. Once we rented the Malibu apartment, going to Maui definitely fell into the category of taking a vacation from a vacation, but we had committed to going to the Maui Film Festival. It was to be a most-expenses-paid trip, and I wasn't about to turn it down.

Maui is my favorite place on Earth. I haven't traveled much (the whole flying thing), but I've been to Maui several times. This wasn't my first time going with Dean, but I hoped it would go a little more smoothly than the last. When I first met Dean I told him how much I loved Maui and that I wanted to go there with him. He wasn't gung ho about the idea because he knew I'd been there with several exes. I told him that if we went together, our new memories would overwrite all my past experiences there. He didn't buy that argument. Finally I said, "Once we get there, you won't think about the exes. It's *Hawaii*. You'll love it." Eventually Dean was convinced, and after Liam was born we planned our first trip to Maui. We booked it months ahead of time. It was an outrageously expensive trip, but Dean and I were celebrating the new success of our show, and I couldn't wait to relax with him on the beautiful beaches and to take walks with him and baby Liam by the ocean.

But our dream vacation wasn't meant to be. By the time the trip rolled around, I was in the first trimester of my pregnancy with Stella and sick as a dog all day, every day. (Not Maui's fault.) It rained the whole time, from the moment we landed till the moment we left. (Bad, Maui, bad.) Dean went diving every day, spending hours underwater—turns out rain doesn't matter as much when you're in an ocean—but it wasn't exactly the trip of my dreams.

I always wanted us to go back. The film festival was perfectly timed—it came right after we finished shooting the fourth season of *Tori & Dean*—and they offered us a good deal: they were paying for our flight and four nights at the Four Seasons; we were paying for Stella's baby nurse, the kids' flights, and the extra nights at the hotel. Our only commitment for the film festival was to attend one party, and it was in the very hotel where we were staying.

In Maui, the night of the film festival, we weren't due down-stairs until ten p.m., an hour past our usual bedtime. The kids were sleeping soundly; Patsy, Stella's baby nurse, was on duty; and Dean and I were lying on the bed, all dressed and ready, watching

TV until it was time to go downstairs to the party. And then who knows what I was doing with my hands or why, but I felt something weird under my armpit. A mass. A lump.

My heart was pounding. What *was* it? Was I imagining things? I felt it again. Something was definitely there. I made Dean feel it. He'd be a voice of reason. Dean said, "Yeah, there's definitely something there. I'm sure it's nothing. Don't worry about it."

Don't worry about it? Hello? I'm a hypochondriac! I invent potential danger and death as a way of being. For all the irrational worries and fears that I lived with every day, here was something actual—a mass that even Dean admitted was there—and he was telling me not to worry. As if that was remotely possible. Shouldn't he be concerned that his beloved wife had a potentially life-threatening tumor? I tried to impress on him the seriousness of the matter.

"I just never thought this would happen to me," I said.

Dean said, "That is so you. You don't even know what it is and you've already written your death sentence."

I was indignant. In my head I hadn't written my death sentence. I mean, maybe in my mind I had breast cancer, which we all knew was life-threatening, but I wasn't saying I was going to die! After all, I'd survived amnesia, a coma, stalkers, and various psychopathic would-be murderer boyfriends—in my made-for-TV movies at least. Okay, I'll admit that maybe I was just indignant because he was saying I was overreacting. But for once I was afraid of something that actually existed. It wasn't some cockamamie fantasy about psychopaths lurking outside dark windows. This time I was confident that I *wasn't* overreacting. I had a malignant lump that was metastasizing as we spoke, and Dean wanted me to relax? Did he even know me?

I lay on the bed, frozen and silent. Dean was no use. He had shut me down. Ordinarily if Dean was unavailable (emotionally or in person) I'd talk to Patsy. Patsy and I had developed a mother-daughter relationship over her years as my children's baby nurse. I knew that she understood the problems I brought to her. She always found a way to comfort me. But Patsy's daughter had died of breast cancer. I couldn't bring it up with her. And I didn't want to call a friend right there in front of Dean, who had just made it clear that he thought it was no big deal. Internally, I stroked my own hair (well, my hair extensions), saying, "It's okay. It's going to be okay."

Finally, after what seemed like a silent eternity, I quietly texted two people: Dr. J, my friend and obstetrician, and Mehran, my gay husband. I wrote, "Oh my God I'm freaking out." I told them about my discovery. Mehran said, "Don't panic, describe it to me, let me talk to my dad." His dad is a doctor. Moments later he texted again to say, "Based on the texture and movement my dad's thinking it's nothing, just a fatty mass." At the same time Dr. J texted, "You're going to be fine, don't worry. You'll come in and see me the day you get back, but I can almost promise you it's fine."

When the time came, Dean and I headed down to the event. I was in heels and makeup but just a casual shift sundress; Maui is beachy and relaxed, and I looked beachy and relaxed on the outside, but inside was a different story. Then the press asked for a photo op. Just what I wanted—the final photo of me before my fatal diagnosis. They asked me to pose with Kristen Bell and Anna Faris. So I stood between them. I was wearing my sundress. They were both wearing sparkly ball gowns worthy of the Golden Globes. I thought, here we are, three cute blond actresses, two of whom are younger, have bigger careers, are wearing fancier dresses, and are presumably lump-free. Perfect. Smile.

As we took those pictures I never stopped thinking, *I have a lump*. As we toasted with champagne: *I have a lump*. I moved my upper arm against it to see if I could feel it. When I went to the bathroom, I checked to see if it was still there. There it was, a hard little reminder that life was in the balance.

There were a few days left before I could go home to be examined by Dr. J. By the light of day I didn't worry too much about the troublesome lump. After the breakfast buffet, Dean and I set up camp next to the kiddie pool. We played in the pool most of the morning. I took Liam down the slide more times than either of us could count. After a poolside lunch, the kids napped, then we all went back to the pool.

I ran into Denise Richards lounging there. She was on vacation with her kids, her best friend, and her father. The last time I'd seen Denise was about a pig.

I guess I should explain about that pig. Right before Stella was born, Dean and I brought Liam to Denise Richards's daughter Lola's birthday party. There was a ridiculously cute pig running around the party. Liam saw the little pig and was really excited about it. Although she certainly already knew it, I said to Denise, "You have a pig!"

She said, "I have a ton of pigs." She took us to the back of the house where, indeed, there were a bunch of pigs running around like chubby, stumpy-legged dogs. I thought they were adorable.

A few months later Denise called to tell me that one of her pigs had given birth. She said, "I remember how excited Liam was when he met the pig. Would you ever consider owning one? They're great pets." Dean and I talked about it. My beloved pug, Mimi La Rue, had recently passed. I wasn't ready to get a new dog. I didn't want Mimi to feel replaced. But I thought a pig might be fun.

We went back to Denise's house. She had some big pigs outside and smaller ones inside. There was a new little pig in a rhinestone collar that I hadn't seen last time. Denise said her name was Stella and that she walked around on a leash like a little lady. I froze at the name Stella. Who had come first—my Stella or this one? I decided not to ask.

Denise showed us a litter of little pigs, all old enough to leave their mother. She picked out one that she thought would grow up to be small—maybe fifteen pounds fully grown—and who had a sweet disposition. She said that the pigs were very smart, friendly, and clean. All we had to do was show him a kitty litter box once, and he'd use it from then on. Denise had a kennel for us, so we brought our little piggy home and named him Milton La Rue, in memory of Mimi.

By the time we got home from Denise's, poor little Milton had shit all over himself in the carrier. Dean gave him a bath in the sink. I thought pigs were supposed to like baths—aren't they supposed to, like, *wallow?*—but Milton was traumatized. He squealed the entire time. I'd never really heard a pig squeal. This wasn't the jolly *oink, oink* that Liam's talking farm puzzle emitted. It was a horrifying, torturous, dying pig scream. I thought my eardrums were going to explode. Our dogs, Chiquita and Ferris, both small dogs but still bigger than Milton, hid under the table, quaking in fear. Milton screamed and screamed. Nothing would comfort or distract him. He was totally freaked out for the duration of the bath and afterward.

After the bath, we brought our new little pig to his room. We were living in our previous house, and—guess where this story is going—we'd just finished decorating it. We gated off a bathroom for Milton and furnished it with a doggie bed and a kitty litter box. We showed him the bed and the box. He looked terrified. He promptly shit all over the bathroom, all over the floor and his bed, everywhere except the kitty litter box. We cleaned it up and showed him the kitty litter box again, but he kept messing up his own space and lying in his own shit.

The next day we took him to the vet. The vet said, "This pig is going to be one hundred pounds."

We said, "No, no. You're mistaken. He's going to be fifteen pounds. Our friend has lots of pigs. She knows." I thought about little Stella-piggy walking around with her stylish collar.

But the vet said, "No, he's going to be big. This pig is a lot of responsibility. Pigs are messy."

"Really?"

"They're pigs."

At home, Milton chased the dogs all over the living room. Ferris was hysterical. Chiquita looked at me reproachfully as if to say, "How could you do this to us?"

I love animals. I rescue animals. I was committed. I would never give up on animals. So I had Dean call Denise.

"We love Milton, but we can't handle him," I heard him saying as I cowered in the next room. She was very gracious and took him back.

Now, in Maui, Denise said that Milton had a really good home. I was happy to hear it, but I knew we'd dodged a giant, everywhere-shitting bullet. I hadn't let guilt and fear of confrontation make the decision for me. For once I'd had the wherewithal to extract myself from a responsibility that was more than I could handle. (Thank God, since I was clearly on the cusp of chemotherapy and pigs would be the least of my worries in the short remainder of my life.) Denise, for her part, was open and pleasant about the whole thing. When she said, "Don't worry about it," I could tell she meant it.

Liam's favorite part of his Maui days came as the sun set. The hotel had a nightly traditional ceremony during which a guy in a grass skirt and headpiece ran through the resort blowing a conch shell and lighting torches. Liam watched him, shouting, "Fire! Fire!" Most of the time after dinner we retreated to our room for our own equally traditional ceremony of watching pay per view, but that night we took the kids to the lobby lounge.

I've been to Maui at many different times in my life, and all of them involved spending time at the lobby lounge in the Four Seasons, which is much more family-friendly than it sounds. As Liam and Stella ran in circles around the bar, someone who worked there looked at Liam and said, "Didn't he sit on the piano here when he was a baby?" and I thought about how I'd been there when I was pregnant with Stella, with nine-month-old Liam sitting on the piano. I'd been single at this bar, with boyfriends, with my brother. I'd been young and drunk at this bar. This bar had seen my whole adulthood. It had suited me as a frolicking twenty-year-old, and now, as Liam and Stella circled the bar stools, I saw that it was actually amazingly family-friendly. The lobby lounge was growing up with me. All the stress of the night before was forgotten as I soaked in the nostalgia.

But that night Dean and I watched *The Haunting in Connecticut,* a horror movie on PPV. The underlying story line was that the main character's son had cancer and moved to Connecticut for treatments. He was sixteen and likely to die. It couldn't be a coincidence. I really did have breast cancer.

At night, in bed, when everyone else was asleep, I was in my head, which was the worst place to be. I'm no stranger to irrational fears and usually I can talk myself down off the wall. I told myself, *I'm only thirty-six; I probably don't have breast cancer.* But the lump was still there. For the first time, my life felt completely out of control. No matter how much I worked or wished or invoked my various talismans, nothing would change the reality of that lump. I had no control over it. There was nothing I could do to make it good or bad news. It was what it was. And because of it, my whole life might change. And then I went down the painful, awful route that every mother must tread at some low point. I thought about how much I wanted to see Stella become a woman. What if I never got there?

I pictured having to videotape messages to Stella that she could play as the years went by. Happy birthday messages for year after year of her childhood. Advice about boys. Hopes for her future. Explanations of the tabloid photos of me humping a reindeer. (Actually, I'll explain that later. For posterity.)

That night in Maui, after watching *The Haunting in Connecticut*, I decided that I was going to live my life differently. If I couldn't control the cancer, I could correct other flaws. It was time to stop thinking I was going to fall off a balcony, crash in a plane, be stabbed in the back in a movie theater or shot through the window of a restaurant. That stuff was irrational. The lump was real. If it was nothing life-threatening, then it had to be a sign that it was time for me to stop living my life in fear. If the lump meant I was dying, well then, I'd balance out that unthinkable truth by living. No more fear of flying. No more walking down the street looking behind myself every second, no more waking the children up every night to make sure they're still breathing, no more checking under my bed every night before going to sleep. No more fatalistic what-ifs, no more irrational fears, no more fear of confrontation. I'd be spontaneous and adventurous. I would book the family a trip to Argentina, no matter the twelve-hour flight. I'd call up the *90210* castmates who weren't speaking to me (more on that to come). I'd try skydiving (okay, who are we kidding?). Except for the cancer, my new life sounded pretty good.

We took a red-eye home and landed at 4:30 in the morning. A few hours later Dr. J sent me in for a mammogram. The doctor immediately saw that it was just a mass. (If the tabloids had known, they would have said, "Too-thin Tori Has Something Fatty—a Mass.") He showed me another one on the other side. He didn't even have to biopsy it. Dean was right. It was nothing. So what if I had real reason to be afraid this time? It was a fight I was happy to lose.

I had promised myself that no matter what the diagnosis was, my lump had changed me. I was a new person. A person who lived life to the fullest. A girl who took life by the balls. The irony in the matter is that if my harmless little lump had actually been cancer, I probably would have experienced a radical shift in the way I faced the world, but it would have been too late. As soon as I found out that I was okay, I went on with my life as it was, irrational fears and all. I didn't change. Not one bit. Isn't that the way it always goes?

Baby Steps

Even if I didn't change my life radically after the scary lump, there was one resolution I made. Actually, it was a notion that was always at the edge of my thoughts, but one that I kept pushing aside, avoiding confrontation as always. Still, if I was going to be honest with myself about what I wanted and needed in my life, there was one thing I knew for sure: I wanted my mother and my children to see each other.

Stella had started saying her first words. Back in May, just before her first birthday, she was sitting in the living room of our old house when she looked up and said, "Mimi, Mimi, *Mimi!*"

Stella and Mimi La Rue's lives only overlapped for a week, and I don't talk about Mimi to the children. I think about her every day, but I don't walk around saying her name. But when Mimi died, a dog psychic told me that she and Stella were connected.

She said, "You'll see, when Stella can speak, she'll know who Mimi is."

I said, "Patsy, did you hear that?"

Patsy said, "Mm-hmm. I heard it."

We have a painting of a pug up on the wall. I carried Stella over to it and showed it to her. She pointed at the dog and said, "Mimi."

Liam was growing up fast too. In September Liam, now two and a half, started going to preschool for three hours, three mornings a week, at the same school where we'd been doing Mommy & Me classes for the past year. Like any mom, I was nervous about leaving him alone at school. He was still so little! The school geared us up for the transition. They told us it was going to be a hard couple of weeks, but that our children would be fine if we "transitioned" them gently. We'd leave them for a little longer every day until they were ready to stay without us for the whole morning. The word *transitioning* made me shudder. It sounded too much like the forced child-to-alien transformation in a sci-fi flick.

Nonetheless, on the first day of school, after about an hour, I told Liam I was going to be gone for a bit. He said, "Okay, bye, Mommy." I stepped out of the room and lingered in the hall with several other mommies. I kept peeking back into the schoolroom, but Liam was always busy playing. I asked the teacher if I should come back in, but she said he was doing fine. For those three hours I waited to see when he would miss me. I desperately waited for the tears, for the teacher to rush out and tell me to come back in because he needed his mommy. I heard other kids crying for their parents, but nothing from my boy. They said that the transition would be harder for the parents than the kids. It was! Those were the longest three hours of my life. Where was the attachment? Where were the tears? He never seemed to notice I was gone.

Finally, when school was over, I went to the main yard. The kids trotted out with their backpacks, Liam last of all. When he finally came running toward me with his little backpack, he looked different. He wasn't my baby anymore. He was a schoolkid.

The next day when I walked him to the room, as soon as we entered he said, "Bye, Mama," and ran off to play with his friends. The teacher smiled and said, "This is good." I returned her smile and walked out, but if this was good, why did I feel so bad? As soon as I was out the door I burst into tears. So much for Liam's separation anxiety. He was already separated. I was the one who was having a tough time separating.

I stayed in the schoolyard the whole day to see if he needed me, half hoping he would, but he didn't. When all the kids came running out with their backpacks on, I knelt down with arms outstretched, but there was no Liam. A little nervous, I went into the classroom. There he was, still playing. The teacher said he didn't want to leave. I said, "Hi, buddy."

"Hi, Mama."

"School's over, you want to go home?"

"Sure, Mama."

And that was it. From then on I went home or to run errands between dropping him off and picking him up. The house felt strangely empty. I had forgotten what it was like to be in a house without Liam. But this was it. For the next eighteen years. During the weekdays my life at home would not include Liam.

Every milestone that Liam passed made me think of my mother. She hadn't laid eyes on Liam since a month before he turned one. She'd never met Stella. Our always-difficult relationship had been aggravated by my books, then her various statements. I'd always felt like I could ignore any and all of our conflict for the sake of Liam and Stella and the relationship I've always wanted them to have with my mother. My mother was their only grandparent, and I knew she was capable of being a loving part of their lives. I wanted them to know her.

Then, that September, I found out my mother was having major surgery on her neck and spine. I couldn't help worrying that something might happen to her during surgery. She hadn't met Stella. Suddenly I felt how much I wanted them to see each other. So I emailed her to see if she could see the kids before her surgery. She happily agreed and we set it up. Our babysitter, Paola, took the kids. I didn't plan to go and I never said that I was coming. But in her emails, when she wrote "looking forward to seeing you and the kids," I wondered if she wanted and expected to see me. Was this her way of reaching out? I didn't want to disappoint her, but I wasn't ready.

Liam came back from his grandmother's house completely obsessed with her. Liam is friendly, but he doesn't form attachments with new people super fast. Still, I wasn't surprised that he and my mother bonded. I've always thought that Liam and my father's souls were connected. It started when I got pregnant with Liam right after my dad passed. The older Liam gets, the more he reminds me of my father in so many ways. He looks like my brother and my dad's side of the family. He listens intently like my father always did, taking everything in. This may not be impressive at two and a half, but he's been that way since he was born. He's also obsessed with movies. Stella can't sit still. She has to be moving and exploring every minute of every day. If I let him, Liam would happily sit in bed with me for an entire day watching movie after movie. And he doesn't zone out. He has a furrowed brow and pursed lips, like he's analyzing the story line and preparing to give notes. He reminds me of Dad watching edits of his shows, minus the pipe. Also, my dad hated to eat. It seemed like a bother to him. Liam's the same way. He's never hungry and has very little interest in eating, no matter how much we beg, while Stella is a garbage face, polishing off her meal, Liam's meal, and our own meals without blinking.

According to their babysitter, Stella was reserved when she met my mother. She was in a cautious phase, so I wasn't surprised to hear that one visit wasn't enough for her to form a real bond. She still had a good day and loved the outing. But apparently, from the minute Liam laid eyes on my mother, they were inseparable. He turned to Paola and said, "Bye bye. Go home," then slid his hand into my mother's. As she showed him the fruit trees in the backyard of the manor, he kept saying, "Grandma carry me! Grandma carry me!" and even though she was about to have back surgery, she kept picking him up.

When it came time to leave, Liam had a full-on meltdown, screaming and clutching her, holding her face with both hands and saying, "No, no! I stay with Grandma." I've never seen him do that to anyone but me and Dean, not even the Guncles (his gay "uncles"). When Paola told me and Dean how Liam had behaved, Dean turned to me and said, "It's your dad." I got a chill.

Liam and Stella came back bearing gifts that my mother had given them. One of them was a stuffed animal. Paola said, "Do you recognize this frog?" According to my mother I had brought this frog to my father when he was recovering from throat cancer.

When my dad died four years ago, my parents and I weren't on good terms, so I didn't have anything of his. My uncle Danny sent me one of his sweaters; it wasn't one of the cashmere V-neck argyles that I remembered him wearing, but at least it belonged to my father. This frog was something of his, something that connected him and me. I was so touched that my mother remembered that, and kept it, and thought to give it to Liam and Stella. Maybe this frog represented our compromise.

A compromise was in order. It was the only hope for peace. My mother's book had come out soon after my second book. Now it was autumn and another book was due to be published. It was Dean's ex-wife Mary Jo's book about getting divorced. The two women with whom I had the most complicated relationships in my life both had books coming out within six months of each other, and I was writing books, and we were all talking about each other instead of to each other. It was surreal.

I'm not going to rehash my mother's book. She said what she said. I said what I said. We both want to move past it and I'm happy about that. And when Mary Jo's book came out, I felt like that was her right. Everyone has their own story to tell. I didn't set out to get involved with a married man and it's definitely not the classiest thing I ever did, but I believe Dean when he says, "If I'd had a great marriage, you could have walked past me naked and I would have said, 'Tori Spelling's hot,' and gone back to whatever I was doing." While I am utterly aware of my role in the end of Dean's marriage and how it isn't exactly a shining example of female solidarity, I don't think of myself as a home wrecker. I'm not sure I even believe in the notion of a home wrecker. I don't think husbands can be stolen. But it is hard and awkward all around.

We all had our books and our reasons for writing them. I didn't want any of it to stand in the way of our children's lives. Just as I want my kids to have a relationship with their grandmother, I want to be a good stepmother to Dean's son Jack, which means smoothing things over with Jack's mother.

Everybody tries, but we're all on tenterhooks, whatever those are. In September, Dean and I went to Jack's first football game of the year. As we walked in, I saw that the elementary school field had three sets of small bleachers with six rows each. They were mostly empty. Some parents were standing up next to the field. I saw Mary Jo sitting in the middle bleacher with her purse by her side. She was alone. I tried to catch her eye, but she was staring straight ahead.

As we entered, I had an instant to decide where I should sit. I was nervous. I wanted to do the right thing, so I tried to put aside all the awkwardness of the situation. We had Jack in common. And besides, I knew her, and she was sitting there. If I put aside the fact I was with her former husband, if I just removed all the complications from the equation, I knew that I would sit with her. That's what you do when you know people.

I plunked myself down next to Mary Jo, just as Dean fanned out past her to the next set of bleachers. Not our most in-sync moment. Now she and I were sitting right next to each other and he was sitting a few yards away. I sat so close that she had to pick up her purse and move it to the other side. I guess I went a little bit overboard; I had the best intentions, but I was so nervous that my heart was pounding. I just wanted to do the right thing.

We said hi and I started talking about Jack. As far as I was concerned, Jack was the point. He noticed everything. It was important that we be civil for his benefit. I smiled and talked to her because I had seen in the past that when we were both there, Jack didn't know how to act toward me. When he saw us interact, he seemed to be more comfortable.

Mary Jo said, "It's a dream come true. I'm a huge football fan. I love the NFL." There it was—a lovely conversation starter. My cue to engage in a harmless conversation about a shared interest. This was, after all, a football game. One problem: I know absolutely nothing about football.

"Oh, that's great, then. You must be so happy that Jack is playing football." They were playing flag football, and Mary Jo was doing her part to keep the conversation going. She was talking about the plays, the linemen, the yard line. I had no idea what any of it meant. I couldn't tell how well Jack was doing or even if his team was winning. I thought I could find something to talk about with any woman, but she had *boy* material. I had nothing to offer. So I was saying things like, "He's doing a great job. Those uniforms are really . . . footbally." It didn't matter if Mary Jo and

I had a deep connection. The point was that we were trying. And I stuck it out the entire game without going on my BlackBerry once.

Back in the spring I had been to a psychic who, unprompted, told me that Mary Jo was going to fall in love, that she was going to find her soul mate. The psychic's predictions were so specific about this guy that I believed everything she said: He was going to be a Canadian living in L.A. He was going to be tall, with dark hair and light blue eyes. They were going to find happiness together. I liked that idea! If she was happy, I'd be happy. Not long after that, at Stella's birthday dinner, Jack had blurted out, "My mom has a boyfriend." I said, "What does he look like?" wondering if this was the soul mate the psychic had seen, but Jack didn't know. But I hoped for that boyfriend. It had to be that the happier she was, the less anger she'd feel toward me. Plus, he sounded cute.

Now, as I sat next to her, I did the girl once-over to assess if there was a boyfriend. Her hair looked nice: she had a fresh blow-out. That was a good sign. She looked fit. Check. She looked tan. Check. Then my lady sleuth skills kicked in. I saw that her toenail polish was chipped. Dead giveaway. No boyfriend. There's nothing embarrassing about the tail end of a pedicure, but if you were courting a new fellow, you'd never let your nails go to pot. Cut me some slack: with no football knowledge and no BlackBerry, I was driven to toenail-level observations.

The game went on, and I sat right next to her, making my best football conversation. Both of us knew full well that she was about to go on a book tour and slam me. It felt like the truce of politics, where opponents shake hands and joke before they tear each other apart in a debate.

A few months later I would be at a family dinner with Dean, Mary Jo, Jack, Liam, and Stella. We went to Emilio's Trattoria. There was a large family sitting at a table near us. It was a really nice dinner, a normal dinner, and nobody watching would know that they were witnessing an ex-wife and a current wife on their best behavior. In fact, I can say for sure that an outside observer would have no idea what was going on; I know because of what happened after we finished dessert. Liam and Stella were running around. Dean and Jack got up to keep an eye on them. Mary Jo and I were alone in the booth. An older woman came over from the next table. She said, "Your children are just beautiful." Clueless to our dynamic, she looked over at Dean and the kids and added, "You two need to make another baby."

Under her breath Mary Jo muttered, "Yeah, right here, right now." Then she looked at me and we laughed. What else could we do?

Mary Jo and I will cross paths until Jack is a grown-up, and even then we will undoubtedly see each other at some of the milestone events in his life. I want us to find a balance. And for all our conflict, I want my mother to be a true part of Liam and Stella's lives. I want them to know her. I want us to find peace. You need to find peace within before you can find external peace. With both my mother and Mary Jo, I knew that I had work to do. I had to do my part to build and keep the relationships.

Make New Friends but Keep the Old

There's the family you're born with, and there's the family you choose. According to my best friend Jenny, the whole trauma of losing my kids to school would be offset by the wonderful new community of moms I was about to discover. Jenny herself had all new friends. The Westside moms. She was always telling me that I'd love them, but instead of looking forward to meeting Jenny's new friends, I just felt jealous.

I've had the same best friends for years: Jenny, Amy, Jennifer, and Sara. The Westside moms were creeping into my territory. Now when I tried to get together with Jenny, it was always, "I can't. Every Tuesday after pickup I have lunch with the Westside moms. You'd love them; they drink wine at one in the afternoon. They're amazing." I didn't like the idea of Jenny having friends I didn't know. Then I finally had a chance to meet one of them in the flesh.

One day Jenny called and said, "I heard you're going to Fox today." Jenny was right; I was going to do an interview for *Fox & Friends*. Jenny had heard about it through her friend Lisa, one of her new Westside mom friends who worked at Fox. Jenny told me that after I did my on-camera interview, I would go backstage and do an interview with Lisa for the web. And Jenny knew as much about it as I did. Hmph.

Jenny was excited for me to meet Lisa, but I was skeptical. Who was this "Lisa" who was monopolizing my best friend? I'd known Jenny since high school. For Halloween once, Jenny, who would have made a perfect Sandy, knew how much it meant to me, so she let me go as Sandy while she spray-painted her hair pink to be Frenchy. The pink didn't come out of her hair for three weeks. She was my best friend. And now I was supposed to share her?

After my on-camera appearance, I went backstage and there she was, the famous Lisa. She was wearing pearls, a knee-length skirt, and a cardigan and looked so . . . grown-up. Was this my new best friend?

As Lisa interviewed me, she was trying too hard to make a connection—maybe as an interviewer, maybe because Jenny had told her we'd love each other. Understandably, she kept throwing in things she knew about me from Jenny to make it more personal. But then she said, "I heard from a little bird that you had a birthday celebration this weekend." That was true, sort of. Dean and I had spent a weekend at Casa del Mar, a hotel that means a lot to us, for my birthday. One of the nights he surprised me by inviting about ten friends to celebrate with us in a cabana at the Viceroy. But the way Lisa said it made it sound like I'd had a full-fledged party, and I had one friend in particular whom I knew would be pissed if she thought she hadn't been invited to a birthday party of mine. That friend would definitely watch this interview, and then I'd be in big trouble.

So when Lisa said that I'd had a birthday celebration, I said "No!" rather vehemently. She looked taken aback, so I quickly backpedaled, "I mean, I had a birthday thing, but it was only ten people, just a few of us."

She said, "Oh, okay," and I could tell she thought I was nuts. Our interview had lost its footing.

Afterwards, I apologized for my overreaction and tried to explain. She said, "I'm so sorry, I didn't know!" That was how we left it, polite and fine, but not exactly the insta-friendship of Jenny's fantasies. So much for me and the Westside moms. Jenny was family that I chose, but I wasn't quite ready for her to expand the clan.

Jenny and my other high school friendships were shifting as we got older, but that was nothing compared to what was going on with my onscreen high school friends, who fell somewhere between the family you're born with and the family you choose. On *90210* there was the infamous I Hate Brenda Club, but who knew that the *90210* gang, my former castmates, had actually formed an I Hate Tori Club?

I've told some of these stories before: Luke Perry dissed me at Jack's birthday party. Ian said on the radio that he was upset by my first book. Shannen came out against its "lies." Even Brian Green, my onscreen/offscreen boyfriend, had nothing nice to say about me. My hairstylist ran into him and said, "Have you seen Tori lately?"

He said, "Oh, I hate Tori." But wait, *why?*

As recently as after I met Dean, Jason Priestley and I were still in email contact. Jason was the one Dean wanted to meet: he's always glad to meet a fellow Canadian. Then when I went to *Dancing with the Stars* to cheer on Ian (this was before the radio incident), Jason wouldn't stand up to give me a hug. I walked across the stage to him, said hi, and bent down to give him a hug, but he wouldn't speak to me. Someone told me they'd seen him in New York having dinner with my ex-husband, Charlie, so I would assume I lost Jason in the divorce, except that he and I had still been in touch after I left Charlie, so loyalty to Charlie didn't explain the cold shoulder. Tiffani Amber Thiessen had definitely sided with Charlie. And she and Jason are close friends. So maybe it was a hand-me-down, belated cold shoulder?

No matter how you slice it, my *90210* castmates, the closest thing to college friends I had, were dropping like flies. The most recent blow came when Dean and I went to get sushi at our local sushi restaurant. I walked in and saw Gabrielle Carteris, who played Andrea. I hadn't seen her in three years, not since the *90210* DVD release party, when I was pregnant with Liam, but there she was, sitting at a table next to the sushi bar, facing me. Our eyes met and I mouthed, "Hi!" across the restaurant. She looked straight down at the table. Awkies. Was it not Gabrielle? Shoot! I couldn't believe the resemblance. The girl across the table looked just like her daughter, but older, around fourteen. Then I realized that her daughter would be about fourteen by now. Wow, we were getting old.

If things weren't awkward enough, they sat us at the sushi bar right next to the table where these people were sitting. I leaned over to Dean and said, "The girl at that table looks exactly like Gabrielle, but it can't be her. She ignored me." Dean glanced over my shoulder, then said, "No, that's definitely Gabrielle Carteris." It looked just like her, unless it was her identical twin.

I asked Dean, "Why would Gabrielle hate me?" I had no idea. Maybe it wasn't her and I was just paranoid.

Dean said, "Well, it makes sense. They all hate you."

Why did they all hate me? I was the most liked person on that set. I was the sweet one. If it was high school (which it pretended to be and in so many ways *was*), I'd have been voted most popular.

I said, "Jennie doesn't hate me." Thank God for Jennie Garth, my sole defender. It was so weird: when we were in high school we acted like grown-ups, but now that we were grown up, it felt like high school. I thought it would be a good idea for us all to go down to the Peach Pit and talk it out over some sodas—that is if Nat, proprietor of the Peach Pit, didn't hate me too.

My gay friends were forming the closest relationships with my children—maybe because my girlfriends had kids of their own to focus on. One nice element of my childhood was that my parents had close friends who were so much like family that we called them aunts and uncles. My girlfriends and I always talked about doing that with our kids. Jenny and I refer to each other as "Aunt Jenny" and "Aunt Tori" to our kids, but it hasn't taken hold. Of all our friends, Liam and Stella have bonded most with Scout and Bill—the Guncles—and Mehran, my gay husband. Calling Scout, Bill, and Mehran "uncle" came naturally. One day I said to Liam, "Mehi's here," and he said, "Uncle Mehi?"

The only thing that kills Mehran is how straight Liam is. One day we were all watching TV and an ad for Barbie came on. Stella gasped in awe. She stared at the screen, mouth open. I said, "That's Barbie."

Stella said, "Barbie! I like it! I like it!"

But Liam said, "No! I fight Barbie."

Mehran said, "Why do you crush my dreams like this?"

The Guncles are a constant in our lives. The kids see them at least once a week, and anytime Dean and I have to both be away, it's the Guncles who fill in as parents. Scout and Bill are mock-competitive over the kids' attention, and I can already see that the kids will play them off each other when they get older. From the start, Liam always wanted Bill to hold him. I think Scout worried that Bill was more "maternal" and would always be the favorite. But then Stella came along and chose Scout. We think Stella bonded with Scout because they both love cheese. When Scout comes in, both kids run up to him and say, "Cheese! Cheese! We want cheese!" Scout says, "That's all they know me for and I'm kind of okay with that." Stella walks right past Bill every time. She chants " 'couty, 'couty," and follows Scout through the house. At school when she picks up the phone and pretends to talk into it, it's always "Uncle Scouty. Hi, Uncle Scouty."

Stella chose Scout, and she chose well. As Scout and Bill go through the process of trying to adopt, Stella made Scout feel wanted and needed just when he's about to become a parent. It's really sweet, especially because I think Stella helped Scout see that Bill isn't the only one with a "maternal" instinct. It's like Stella was telling him that he could do it. It was just what Scout needed. Stella is helping create harmony without knowing it.

My friends are my found family. We're on the phone, texting, rearing our children together the way I always imagined. There are shifts as our lives change direction and as our children grow. We're always going to meet new people and make new friends. Some people say that celebrities have trouble finding real friends. There are too many hangers-on and users to sort out the wheat from the chaff. I get that. But I think maybe what's harder is finding a normal rhythm with people who recognize you before you even meet. It's been hard for me, anyway. And it's not just people acting odd; it goes two ways. It's my fault too. At Liam's school I met a couple of other moms that I liked. They came over to my house for Halloween. Later in the night we were supposed to meet up with another school mom for trick or treating, but in the chaos of Halloween it got to be too late. One of my new mom friends said, "Just send her a text. She won't care." But her husband, an actor, knew better. He chimed in, "Of course she cares. She told all her friends that Tori Spelling might show up." It was exactly what I feared but could never quite express about new friends. Did they like me, or were they interested in "Tori Spelling"?

At a holiday party at Liam's school, one of the moms invited us to a playdate. It was to be just the boys in his class and their moms. I said, "I'd love to come. I want Liam to have more play-dates."

She said, "Don't worry, my son just went to his first birthday party." We were all in the same boat, looking to form friendships for our kids with families we liked hanging out with.

On the day of the playdate I had two appointments on the other side of the hill, but I was determined that Liam and I would make it. And I wanted to go without Dean—to prove to myself that I could do it alone.

I raced home from the doctor. It was only a two-hour play-date and I was forty-five minutes late. This threw me a little, but I wasn't daunted. When we arrived the moms were in the kitchen chatting and the kids—about six of them—were play-ing in another room while the dad of the house watched over them.

The moms were in the middle of a conversation. As far as I could tell they were talking about starting small businesses. I wanted to chime in—I have businesses; I should have something to contribute!—but I didn't know what to say. So I just sat there, trying to look friendly and open.

The hour or so passed quickly. I hadn't made any impression, good or bad, but that was okay. It was all very low-key. Soon the moms started making moves to leave. It was time for our sons' naps. Another one of the moms was leaving, so I said, "I'll walk out with you." She and I went to the playroom, where Liam was deeply absorbed in playing with the kids' kitchen. I said, "Liam, time to go."

Liam said, "No, thank you," and continued to play. The other mom gathered her stuff, picked up some toys, and she and her child waited for me as I tried to cajole Liam into leaving.

I said, "Liam, it's really time to go now." No response. This was taking too long. My mom friend was waiting and the other moms were gradually trickling out the front door. I didn't want to be the guest who overstayed.

Then the other mom said, "Oooh, I think he pooed." She was right. Liam needed a diaper change, but in my hurry I'd left the diaper bag in the car.

I said, "It's okay, we're on our way home."

She said, "Do you need a diaper? We can ask the mom. I'm sure she has a diaper to fit Liam."

I said, "No, it's fine." I didn't want to go out to the car or to bother the mom. We'd be home soon anyway.

She said, "You're going to let him sit in shit?"

I said, "We live two blocks away. He'll be fine."

She pressed me. "Really?"

I said, "Yeah! Don't judge me!" I said it lightly, like I was kidding. And I was, kind of.

She said, "No, I'm not."

I said, "Come on, Liam." I picked him up. But Liam was really enjoying this playdate and was absolutely not ready for it to end. He started screaming and crying. I carried his writhing form to the door.

The host mom said, "Thanks for coming, Liam." My son was howling and arching his back as I tried to hold him. The mom kindly tried to reason with him, telling him he could come back for another playdate soon.

Liam pointed his finger in her face and said, "No, shut up, don't talk to me." I was horrified.

I said, "Liam, we don't talk to people that way." At that he slapped me in the face. My glasses flew off my face. My knit beret slid to the side. I was too shocked to do or say anything. Then he started choking me. Liam had never done this before.

The mom said, "Don't hurt your mom, that's not nice."

Then, instead of reining Liam in the way I should have, I just started laughing, an awkward, nervous laugh. I turned to the mom and said, "I don't know why I'm laughing. I'm sorry. Thank you, we had a great time." With that, I tumbled out the door, screaming poopy child in arms, glasses in hand, hat askew. Well, I guess I had made an impression after all.

Our first playdate with school moms. My child acted up, told our host to shut up, and attacked me at the door. I was never going to be invited back. I finally had a little group of mom friends and they were all going to hate me. I could imagine the phone calls they were trading even as Liam and I arrived home. "Tori Spelling's really nice, but she has no control over her child. We don't want him hanging out with our kids."

That night I composed a thank-you email apologizing for the scene. I saved it for a day, deleted it, rewrote it, then finally sent it. It said, "We had a great time, thanks. It was a perfect day except for Liam pummeling my face as we walked out. How embarrassing." Then I waited, hoping for the breezy response that would assure me we hadn't been blacklisted forever. It never came.

Jenny, Mehran, Amy, Sara, Jennifer, and I have known each other for so long and play such specific roles in each other's lives that we are irreplaceable. Nobody else will ever know us in the same way. I count myself lucky to have my old friends, my hand-picked family. Our relationship has nothing to do with celebrity. They aren't alerting their friends when I might attend a party. I don't have to worry about whether they think I'm changing my son's diaper quickly enough. I don't have to prove myself as a mother. We are simply friends, there for fun and when we need each other. And I was about to need them more than ever.

In Sickness and in Health

One of the most important members of my found family is Patsy, who was first Liam's baby nurse, then Stella's. When Stella turned one in June, Patsy's job was finished. A couple of weeks later she headed home to Waleska, Georgia. I hated to see her go, but I knew I'd see her soon enough. The plan was for her to come back at the beginning of October to have gastric bypass surgery. We'd helped her to arrange the surgery—I sent her to my internist, who found her a doctor—and the doctor was here in Los Angeles. But then Patsy got sick. Her doctor in Georgia said that she wasn't getting enough oxygen because of her weight. Because she wasn't getting enough oxygen, he didn't think it was safe for her to fly to L.A. She needed to have the surgery right away, and she needed to have it in Atlanta.

After I got off the phone with Patsy, Dean came into the room. He immediately saw from my face that something was wrong. I told him that it felt weird to me that she was having surgery without me. We'd planned it together. I never imagined I wouldn't be there to help her through it. Dean didn't hesitate for a moment. He said, "I'll just go get her. I'll drive across the country and bring her back here." Leave it to Dean, my hero, to rise to the moment. Patsy is like family, and I loved that Dean saw her that way too. As we thought it through, we realized that of course it made more sense for Patsy to stick with her new Atlanta doctor and for us to go to her. We started making plans for a trip across the country.

Then, at the end of September, a week or two before we were due to leave for Patsy's bedside, I myself got sick. Dean, Liam, and Stella all had a stomach flu, but mine was different. I had severe stomach pain and an unrelenting headache. I wound up in the hospital. There I was, stuck in the hospital when I was supposed to be heading east to Patsy's side. I felt horrible. I'd gone through the whole process with Patsy, every step of the way. I went to every doctor's appointment with her. I tried to get her healthy through eating right and taking walks. I promised I'd be there with her. If she wasn't having the surgery in L.A., I wanted to be there. If I couldn't be there for the surgery, I wanted to be there right afterward.

Instead I lay in my hospital bed in so much pain that I felt like I'd been stabbed in the stomach. I couldn't breathe. It was gut-wrenching. Doctors did test after test but all were inconclusive. They couldn't figure out what was wrong with me. It was like being on an episode of *House* (and not as a special guest star). The gastrointestinal specialists were looking up rare stomach diseases in textbooks. Finally my gastroenterologist said, "Do you think it could be stress? Stress can manifest itself as a real problem."

I glanced toward the foot of the bed. There lay a tabloid magazine that Dean had brought me for some light pleasure reading. Inside it I knew there was an article saying that I weighed ninety-five pounds and was in the hospital because of Mary Jo's newly released book, *Divorce Sucks,* and the stress that it was putting on Dean's and my relationship. Was stress the root of my stomach issues? I shrugged. "Possibly."

Mary Jo's book certainly wasn't the source of all my stress. All summer the tabloids had run stories on two rumor tracks: my allegedly troubled marriage and my alleged anorexia. Both stories were untrue and hurtful, but the relationship rumors were far more outrageous and offensive because we knew exactly who the source was and he had once been our friend.

When Dean and Mary Jo were still married, they moved to California without knowing many people. Jack started school, and they became friends with some of the other parents, including one couple in particular, Mike and his wife. When Dean and I met, fell in love, and came back to Los Angeles, he went on a previously scheduled trip to Palm Springs with his family and Mike and his family. Then Dean left Mary Jo, and we didn't know what the fallout would be. But for the most part the other parents Dean was friends with accepted me. The school moms invited me to an all-girls lunch. They seemed happy for Dean. Even Mike and his wife, who had been with Mary Jo at the hardest moment and had good reason to spurn me, were friendly and welcoming. The four of us went out for double dates. We spent holidays together. They helped us look for our first house. When we found one, Mike helped us move in.

Then one day the three of us—Dean, Mike, and I—were out together at a little coffee shop in Beverly Hills. This was before the news about the end of my marriage and the start of my relationship with Dean had broken (well, the *Enquirer* had run a story, but it had passed without the rest of the press taking notice). But now, while we were having coffee, the paparazzi appeared at the parking structure directly across the street as if they knew where to find us. This was a big deal. We were doing our best to lay low, and it hadn't been hard. At that time the paparazzi didn't follow us everywhere; it was something of a paparazzi lull in my life. So where had they come from? How did they know where to find us? Had Mike tipped them off? We couldn't be sure, but Dean talked to Mary Jo about our concerns. Ultimately we stopped being friends with him and his wife, and Mary Jo moved back to Toronto, so their friendship dropped off as well.

Then recently Mary Jo moved back to L.A. We heard through Jack that she had picked up her friendship with Mike and his wife again. The two families were together every weekend. But time had passed. Besides, it wasn't exactly our business who Mary Jo was friends with anyway.

When Mary Jo moved into her new house in L.A., Dean helped furnish Jack's room. He bought Jack a bed, a desk, new curtains. Then Mary Jo decided that Jack needed an armoire since the room didn't have a closet. She told Dean that she wanted to hire Mike to build it. This made sense: Mike had always done construction on the side. In fact, he and Dean had done some construction jobs together. Dean told Mary Jo that he'd pitch in to pay for half the armoire.

A while later, Dean got an email from Mike asking for money for the armoire. Dean explained, "This is between you and Mary Jo. I told her what I'd contribute." Mike persisted and started to get personal, rehashing things from when Dean and I first met. Dean stopped responding to Mike and called Mary Jo to remind her that they'd had an agreement about how much he would contribute to the cost of the armoire. He told her that she'd have to work things out with Mike.

Three weeks to the day after Dean and Mike's final exchange, there was a front-page article in *Star* magazine with the headline, "Inside Tori's Loveless Marriage. Best pal tells all." And there it was, inside *Star,* a photo of Mike and Dean, arm in arm. Mike didn't even try to hide that he'd given the magazine the story. He quoted Dean as saying that I had the face of a horse and that marrying me "was going to be good for my career. I'm going to have millions now." It was hard-core. Really shitty stuff. Was that stressful enough to give someone severe stomach problems? I'll say.

If that weren't enough, Mike had given *Star* snapshots of me that had been taken at his family's Christmas party during the six months that we were friends. A bunch of us were standing on his front lawn. He'd put a wire reindeer out on the lawn. I was tipsy and we were all joking around. I can't have been the only one who thought it would be funny to pretend to hump the reindeer. Now here it was, his photo of me humping a reindeer like a girl gone wild.

The whole article was so boldly outrageous that I had to wonder if there was anything to it. I said to Dean, "Is it at all possible that you ever maybe said something to him that he maybe misconstrued, like 'At least I'll always have money to support Mary Jo and Jack' or anything like that?"

Dean said, "No way." But that didn't matter. From the day that article appeared, through the rest of the summer, every magazine was obsessed with our "loveless" marriage. No, not stressful at all.

When these stories come out, Dean always wants to say something. But my publicist always tells us, "Say nothing. If you say nothing, it goes away faster." So we didn't make a statement. I tweeted about it, saying "*Star* magazine says we have a loveless marriage." I told my tweeps not to believe it. Dean did something similar. But the injustice lingered.

Was it a coincidence that Mary Jo's book, *Divorce Sucks,* was published a few weeks after the *Star* article? The article mentioned her and the forthcoming book and included a photo of her with Jack as a baby (though the caption said it was Lola, Jack's adopted sister). A few weeks later *Star* had the exclusive on excerpts from Mary Jo's book, which they ran three weeks in a row. Which was also not stressful in the least. It was like a weekly massage.

In the middle of all of this, Jack went home to his mother's backyard Labor Day party. One of the guests was Mike. A month later I was in the hospital for my stomach.

The loveless marriage story was only half the tabloid trouble. Before they bought Mike's story, *Star* had decided that I had anorexia. They ran a few stories about it and the other tabloids followed suit. I took all the negative commentary about my weight to heart. I wasn't starving myself. When I made an effort to lose the baby weight, my body just kicked back in. I returned to the same weight I'd been before I had babies. People had seen me pregnant for two years. They might not remember, but I've naturally always been super tiny.

People didn't think they were being insulting when they told me I looked too thin. For the record: "too thin" is not a compliment. It may be more socially passable than "too fat," but to me it said something was wrong with the way I looked. Maybe I'd gone too far when I tried to lose the baby weight. Maybe I *was* too thin. I didn't have an eating disorder. But I decided I could stand to gain five or ten pounds. So that summer in Malibu I let myself eat whatever I wanted. I had fun. I gained weight and outgrew my tiniest jeans. I was kind of proud that I'd gained weight. I knew I wasn't too thin anymore.

During the summer all the tabloids were obsessed with my weight, and then it died down. Then came the pictures of me humping a reindeer and the loveless marriage. That became the new big news. Then that died down too. But when I went into the hospital, it all started up again. I was ninety-five pounds and living a loveless marriage all over again. My publicist says that I started it by tweeting about my health. She told me not to tweet about my health anymore. Instead of taking her wise advice (Sorry, Jill!), I got mad at the tabloids. One week I'd seen the same photo in two magazines. One magazine said, "Tori's anorexic," and the other magazine wrote, "Look how fab this mom looks!" Then the next week that magazine had joined the anorexic chorus. I wanted to call them to say, "But last week you thought I looked great!"

So now, just after I was released from the hospital, I lashed out at *Star* magazine in my own not-very-aggressive way by tweeting that they should check their facts. I wrote, "They should come weigh me. I weigh 107 pounds."

I'm honestly not hung up about my weight. I'm not anorexic. But 107 wasn't my actual weight. My scale said I weighed 104. But *Star* said I was 95 pounds. Nine pounds didn't seem like a big-enough difference, so I added a few pounds; 107 sounded like a good number. Nobody would make up 107.

The next day I got an email from my publicist saying, "How should I respond?" (So professional, she chose not to remind me that I brought this on myself.) Attached was an email from *Star* magazine saying, "We want to take up Tori on her weight challenge. When can we come weigh her?" Shit. Now I was busted.

I'd been out of the hospital for a week. When I got the email from my publicist I was on my way to my gastroenterologist for a follow-up visit. Emails had been flying back and forth all day between *Star* and my publicist. She was saying, "Tori's fine. She's healthy." So by the time I went into the doctor, I was feeling very sensitive about the whole weight issue.

I'd been to this doctor twice before for my stomach problems, and each time the same nurse had weighed me. This time she said, "We can get your weight or we don't have to." Why was she offering me a choice? Had she read the tabloids? Did she think I had an eating disorder? Enough!

I let forth a defensive stream: "Why would you not want to

take my weight? Don't you take everyone's weight? I'm not different. You can take my weight." The poor nurse looked terrified. I was a crazy person.

Defiantly, I took off my boots and got on the scale. It said 103. Then the nurse wrote down 101 on my chart. I said, "Why'd you put one-oh-one?"

She stammered, "Two pounds for clothing . . . ? "

I said, "Two pounds! But I took off my boots. I'm wearing leggings. I didn't even wear a bra today, for God's sake!"

The poor nurse—she was going about her day, doing what she always did, and I was attacking her, a complete psycho. She said, "Don't worry about it. Most people like when I take their weight down a couple of pounds."

I backpedaled, back to my meek, overpolite self. "Oh, you're right. Okay, thanks."

As I drove home, my publicist called. She said, "So, what did the scale say? If it's one-oh-seven, we can send it to *Star* and the whole thing will be resolved."

I said glumly, "It wasn't the right weight."

While I was in the hospital, I was in pain, I missed Patsy's surgery, and the tabloids had (another) field day speculating on my afflictions. But for all that, the hospital was kind of nice. They had excellent mac 'n' cheese, which I ordered every night. I watched soaps, *Oprah,* and *The View.* It was very relaxing, although I will confess that I was a little annoyed to see that Heidi Montag was cohosting *The View.* When I had cohosted a year or two earlier,

I felt like I'd been handpicked, that I was being groomed to be a talk show host. Now I watched the show for two days in a row and saw first Heidi Montag, then Khloe Kardashian cohosting. Apparently the bar for guest hosts wasn't fantastically high. So much for my talk show host fantasies. And Heidi got to cohost when Barbara Walters was there. She sat right next to her. Barbara Walters wasn't present when I cohosted. That added envy to my disappointment.

During my convalescence Mehran visited; Jenny visited. Bill and Scout came in as I was being wheeled into my room after a battery of tests. Sticking out from behind the closed curtains I saw a pair of white stockinged feet lying on the bed. As I rolled closer I saw that it was Bill decked out in a costume. He was a nurse-stripper. Scout was next to him, wearing a doctor costume. They'd gone to such lengths to cheer me up, but the truth is I was in good spirits. If stress was the root of my stomach pain, well, the hospital was the perfect place to recover. I was sleeping more than I ever did at home. I was taking a break from my BlackBerry. I had my weeklies and my soaps. Dean stayed with me every night. It was much more relaxing than Malibu. Pitiful though it was, the hospital was my real vacation.

Just Tori

Patsy's surgery had happened without me, but as soon as I got out of the hospital, all the McDermotts embarked on a pilgrimage to Patsy. Seeing Patsy was the point, but I'd always imagined driving across the country with my family while the kids were still young. I definitely wanted to stop everywhere to shop, but I mainly loved the idea of taking two weeks to decompress, to just be a mom traveling with my family without flying. We would make scrapbooks, full of leaves and souvenirs and crafts we made along the way. It would be a trip that we could repeat, a tradition that would grow with the kids. The Guncles signed on right away, our film crew decided to come along, and we were off.

Our first stop was Peggy Sue's 50's Diner in Yermo, California. Peggy Sue's was an original restored diner with a huge collection of Hollywood memorabilia, a "dinersaur" park, and the vast souvenir shop of my dreams. Peggy Sue, a former starlet, and her husband, Champ, run the place. We ate, shopped in the souvenir shop, visited the dinosaur sculptures, fed the ducks in the duck pond, then walked to the parking lot. As we approached our RV, a huge tour bus pulled up and ejected a pack of about fifty tourists, all with cameras. One middle-aged woman waved frantically at me, shouting "Tori! Over here! Tori!" I turned and smiled. Fifty cameras bobbed up all at once. I waved at them. Then the first woman came closer and whispered, "Nobody here knows who you are but me."

I said, "Oh, that's okay. I'm just Tori." I smiled and posed for all the tourists who had no idea who I was, then climbed into the RV, where Scout was in hysterics. Between gasps he said, "A bunch of people want to take your picture—so flattering—but someone has to ruin it by telling you that nobody has any idea who you are. That's your life in a nutshell!"

When we planned the trip east, we researched stops along the way that seemed kitschy and kid-friendly, so our next major stop was not far from Peggy Sue's—a place on Route 66 called Stewart's Petrified Wood in Holbrook, Arizona. It was a quirky place that sold petrified wood, meteorites, and dinosaur bones. Scattered through the desert land were large plaster tepees and, incongruously, more of the dinosaur sculptures that were emerging as a tourist trap phenomenon. So random. This place also had an ostrich farm. I couldn't help picturing the owners sitting on some porch, drinking beer, watching the sun set, and coming up with the next crazy feature to lure drivers roadside.

In the shop we were welcomed by a funky-looking character named Gazelle. She showed us beautiful polished meteorites that looked like sliced agate and cost over $500. As soon as I saw the price tags, I picked Liam up. I couldn't believe that people driving along the highway would drop big bucks on these rocks, but Gazelle told me that "everyone" came there. Tom Cruise had stopped by, Jerry Seinfeld had bought one of her meteorites, and she was bringing in a million dollars a year. I was impressed. That sounded like good business to me. I told Gazelle that I might try to find some meteorites and go into the meteorite business for myself. She got all worked up and said, "You're funny. I want you to live next door to me. You could be my neighbor." Then she saw me looking at agate bookends and said, "I like you. I'm going to give you a discount. I like you and you're funny." She sold me the $250 bookends for $75.

Then some more customers came in and I heard Gazelle saying to them, "I like you. I'm going to give you a discount because I like you."

I felt betrayed. When the other travelers left, I said to her, "I thought you liked me, Gazelle. I thought we had something special. Then you went and said the same thing to those people."

Gazelle said, "Maybe I liked them too."

In addition to the bookends, I bought some arrowheads and pieces of what Gazelle told me was petrified dinosaur poo for Liam and Stella's scrapbooks. Then we went out to the ostrich farm, where Dean held out Liam's hand to help him feed the ostrich. I watched in silence, impressed and horrified at the same time. I never would have allowed that perfect little hand near that unpredictable beak.

Then, as we were leaving the ostrich farm, a couple walked in.

It was an older couple, both with gray hair. As soon as I saw the woman, I gasped. Oh my God, she looked exactly like Dean's mother. I never had a chance to meet Dean's mother—she died when he was fifteen and she was in her fifties—but I'd seen many pictures. I was certain that this was exactly what she would have looked like as an older woman if she'd lived longer. It took my breath away. I couldn't stop staring at her. They were identical.

We were wrapping up our visit. Dean was already in the RV with the kids. Scout, Bill, and I were finalizing our purchases. I told Bill and Scout about Dean's mother. They thought I should bring Dean out to see her, but I wasn't sure. What if he didn't see the resemblance? Would it bother him that I was presuming to recognize his mother, the mother I'd never met?

I decided I couldn't let this opportunity pass. I went to the RV to get Dean. As I led him back to the shop I said, "I could be totally wrong, please don't get mad at me, but there's a woman here who reminds me of your mother." I brought him to her and we started chatting. She and her husband had an RV too. They collected something—rocks or stones—and ran a business. I asked if we could take a picture with them and they agreed. Then we went back to our RV. I said to Dean, "What did you think?"

He said, "Yeah. Wow. It's different, because she doesn't have a Canadian accent, but her face looks exactly like my mom." He wasn't angry, but he also wasn't as excited or emotional as I was. For me it was like she'd come back from the dead, but it didn't feel like that for him since he (obviously) knew her so well in life. But later we'd have reason to think twice about this woman and what that short encounter meant in our lives. It had been a full first day.

Our first night we went to a motel. It was my first time staying in a cheap motel. (I've stayed at resorts where you enter your bungalow through an outside door, but those are fancy resorts. I'm pretty sure they don't count.) And at $29.99 per night, I'm pretty sure it was the least amount of money I've ever spent to stay anywhere, including my own house if you amortize the mortgage.

The kids were fine. They could sleep anywhere. The same wasn't true for me. All I know about motels I learned from the movie *Psycho*. The friendly guy at the front desk—wasn't he a little *too* friendly? But I was game. This was part of the adventure. I wanted to see America. Until we got to our room. The air conditioner was a box sitting on the rug. Next to the box was a stain that looked like blood. What else could it be? It had to be blood! I pointed it out to Dean. He laughed and said, "Stay here while I grab the luggage?" I nodded and gulped.

The door closed behind Dean. As I stood in the doorway my vision panned from the bloodstain over to the kids. They were on the bed, rolling on the comforter like happy puppies. How cute . . . Holy crap, the comforter! I'd seen *Dateline* or some other show talking about the skankiness of hotel comforters. They were worse than a communal bowl of after-dinner mints. My children were probably playing in a germ pit of fecal matter and dried semen (no offense to Motel 6). I grabbed Stella and Liam and snatched the comforter out from under them, throwing it in a heap in the corner.

Then I turned on the TV. Big mistake. The movie playing was *Identity*, with John Cusack, in which ten strangers are stranded at a hotel in Nevada and murdered one by one. There was John

Cusack, coming out of a motel room that looked exactly like ours. Oh, come on! Couldn't the motel somehow control what was showing on their channels so as not to frighten the patrons? The same way airplanes never show airplane disaster movies? I was trying to be a grown-up, but this was beyond. By the time Dean returned with the luggage, I was in full panic. Stifling my fear, I put the kids to sleep. Then I climbed into our bed with all my clothes and socks on. I looked up at the ceiling. What was that on the ceiling? Blood. I was certain it was blood. Could it get any worse? I huddled there in sleepless terror for the rest of the night.

Now we were headed to Dallas, my father's hometown. On our way we stopped in Amarillo, Texas, to visit the world-famous Big Texan Steak Ranch, where we wanted to attempt the world-famous 72-ounce steak challenge. As they say at Big Texan, "Many have tried. Many have failed." In order to earn our 72-ounce top sirloin steaks and a place of honor on the list of world-famous challenge winners, we had to eat a fried shrimp cocktail, a salad, a baked potato, a dinner roll, and the entire megasteak in under an hour.

Dean ordered his steak medium and it came to the table dry and tough, cooked to the bone. Dean didn't flinch. As always, he was a total competitor. He stopped talking to us and focused one hundred percent on the task at hand. Going primal, he started tearing long strips of steak off with his hands, standing up and stomping around to aid digestion. Meanwhile I was making jokes, hiding the shrimp, and shoving my dinner roll down my bra.

Later in the dinner I started feeling guilty about the hidden dinner roll. I wasn't a cheater. And besides, what if a reporter from *Star* magazine was in the corner of this Amarillo, Texas, steakhouse watching and preparing to bust me for cheating and/or hoarding food because of my alleged eating disorder? I pulled the roll out and ate it after all.

I probably ate eight ounces of steak—more than Scout!—but I barely made a visible dent in the plateful. Meanwhile Dean scarfed fifty-six ounces. A mere sixteen ounces short of the great glory. Alas, it was not meant to be. Stuffed and defeated, we paid for our meals and headed to Dallas.

In Dallas we met up with my eighty-year-old cousin Sam, the son of my father's oldest sister, Becky. I'd met Sam only twice: once when my family went to Dallas by private train when I was three and not again until he came to my wedding to Charlie. Now, in Dallas, I asked Sam to show me and Dean where my father had grown up—the house he lived in on Browder Street. Sam pointed out where my father's house had been. It was a sleazy motel now, but his elementary school was still down the block.

My cousin Sam showed up with a copy of my father's memoir, some of the pages marked. He was clearly a Spelling: he came ready to give notes, in this case not on a script but on a life. Sam told me, "When your father left Texas, he tried to forget Dallas." I didn't remember it that way at all. He'd always told me stories about how he was too poor to buy shoes; how he brought home leftover bread from the bakery; how he ran home from school, trying not to get his ass kicked for being Jewish. But Sam said, "Aaron told stories that put Dallas down." Where my father told

Escape 2 Malibu

Mama and her Malibu Babes.

My little man is ready for the rays.

Chillin' in the 'bu.

Ladies who luau.

Three tickets to Paradise.

Hula hottie.

Magical Maui

Stella giving tough love.

Monkey's first day of school . . .
my baby is all grown up!

Hats off to Guncle Scouty.

Guncle Billy makes
the best pillow!

Our Pedal to the Metal Papa.

The whole gang RV style.

There's no place like home.
No, really.

Liam and I get our kicks—and Slim Jims—on Route 66.

Stella, meet diner pie.

Eating my
weight in steak.

The rumors are
true—I have
gotten smaller.

Patsy's girl . . .

and her boys (Gays on loan!).

stories of his poor childhood, Sam wanted to remember the love and laughter. He said, "I thought we were the luckiest kids in the world." I think Sam felt like my dad abandoned the family to build a life of success and fortune in L.A. My opinion was that the storyteller in my father saw the dramatic appeal of his remarkable change of circumstances, his rags-to-riches tale, but I can see how his relatives may not have been thrilled about that portrait.

I just said, "My dad always spoke fondly of Texas." Sam seemed surprised and glad to hear that. He showed me family photos I'd never seen before and took me to my grandparents' gravesite.

There they were, David and Pearl Spelling, my grandparents. My middle name is Davey after my grandfather David Spelling, but I met my father's parents only once, when I was three. They died soon after. On the other side, my maternal grandmother died when I was five. The only grandparent who was around when I was growing up was my mother's father, but I always missed having a grandmother. It was part of why I wanted my children to have a relationship with my mother. I took a leaf from each gravesite for Liam and Stella's scrapbooks.

Here was another side effect of my father's fear of flying. Because we rarely traveled, I always felt like I had a small family. Going to Dallas made me realize for the first time that I actually had a large extended family. I wished I'd had a chance to get to know everyone while we were growing up. The family history was dying out and I, at least, couldn't do much to sustain it now.

When we left Texas, we had a long drive east to Mississippi. As the miles of highway rolled past, Dean's and my true road trip selves emerged. Dean, who has a tendency to get completely consumed by new interests, particularly if they involve driving manly vehicles (witness his motorcycle obsession), got extreme about driving the RV. At the very first truck stop we hit, Dean bought truck gloves, a steering wheel cover, and weights that he could use to build strength in one arm while driving with the other. Each morning he made an enormous cup of coffee, put on a headset to listen to a CD (at one of the truck stops I got him two CDs, a *Life on the Highway* compilation and *Greatest Country Hits*), and climbed up into the driver's seat as if he were driving a big rig.

Once Dean had assumed his trucker role, there was no interacting with him. He was in character. A Method trucker. When I tried to engage him, he grunted sentence fragments: "Precious cargo. Must stay focused. Eyes on the road." You didn't have to have a special license to drive the RV, but a couple of guys on our film crew actually had commercial driver's licenses. They could have given Dean a break. Even the executive producer offered to drive if Dean got tired, but nope. He wouldn't hear of it. He insisted on driving the entire way himself. It was so Dean.

Meanwhile, I found my own new obsession: truck stops. Okay, I guess I'll concede that my obsession fell under the larger category of "shopping," which meant it was anything but new to me. But it was certainly a new subcategory. I never knew there was such a thing as a truck stop, but before we left, Dean explained to me that truck stops were like giant 7-Elevens, stocked with every junk food imaginable, trucker souvenirs, and a wide selection of hats with slogans. He had me at junk food. Dean never wanted to linger. He had a certain number of miles he wanted to cover every day (of course), and we were always behind schedule. But when he was forced to stop for gas, Liam and I would dash into the truck stop for a little taste of America.

If I went quickly, head down, grabbed my Cheetos, and hurried out, I could do a truck stop without getting recognized. But most of the time I wanted to scrutinize the aisles. People would stop, do a double take, then stare at me. I don't think anyone expected to run into me at a truck stop in the middle of the United States. People were shocked. They touched me a lot, as if to confirm that I was real.

We found un-PC hats about shooting ducks and eating deer. There was a stuffed animal lion's head trophy to decorate the RV. I bought a sign that said, "What happens on the road stays on the road." And Liam and I got seriously into pork rinds.

There were long driving days in the RV. Dean drove while I did crafts with the kids. Before we left home I'd made a craft box for each kid. I put in homemade play dough, pipe cleaners, googly eyes, stickers, crayons, and paper. The play dough was a huge hit. We made farm animals using the pipe cleaners and googly eyes. We put stickers on each other's faces. We read books, sang songs, and watched DVDs. The kids slept a lot.

Before I knew it we were rolling into Atlanta. The trip had been work; entertaining the kids in a small place is hard enough. With big cameras taking up critical room, space was pretty tight. And Dean was in such a myopic trucker trance that we barely spoke for the entire trip. When we finally arrived in Atlanta, I said, "Hi! I miss you and I've been in an RV with you for almost a week."

Dean said, "Well, we were on the clock. I had to get you here safely."

Now that we were here, intact, we were ready to fulfill our goal. We were all excited to see Patsy.

It had been two weeks since Patsy's surgery, which had gone well. She knew we were coming, but we wanted to surprise her anyway, so we hid at her sister Joan's house. Dean, the kids, Scout, Bill, and I were all there to meet her. My friend James, who's a designer, had come separately to help us with a surprise for Patsy. And Mehran was there too. He flew in to see Patsy and be part of the surprise. All of my friends have been with Patsy through the past few years, hearing her stories and knowing how much she wanted this surgery. They wanted to be there with her as she moved on with her life.

As Patsy walked in the front door, the first thing she had to see was the *Tori & Dean* camera, there to catch (and spoil) her surprise. But Patsy walked in, saw the camera, and just kept walking. She'd been with us long enough to know the drill. Cameras don't count. No matter what the circumstances, you pretend they aren't there. Patsy was cool. She didn't flinch or react to the cameras in the slightest. I thought, *I've taught her well.* Then we jumped out, all wearing "Team Patsy" T-shirts. When she saw all of us, she gasped, "Oh!" We'd surprised her in spite of the camera.

Patsy always says that the babies forget her when she leaves, but both Liam and Stella ran right over to hug her.

Our planning for the trip wasn't all about hitting the best truck stops on the way. After we'd all spent some time together, I said to Patsy, "I have a surprise for you. You have a phone reading with

John Edward." John Edward is a psychic. On his TV show, *Crossing Over with John Edward,* he helps his audience members communicate with people on the other side. Patsy and her husband, Humphrey, had raised six children, but the great tragedy of her life was that the three oldest had died. Patsy has always wanted to meet John Edward. It's one of her dreams—to communicate with the children she loved so much and lost. I knew that after her surgery she'd have a new lease on life, and it seemed like the right time to try to get her a reading. I talked to my publicist, and through her John agreed to do a phone reading with Patsy, and while he was at it, he'd do it for me and Dean too.

Patsy was so excited. She and her daughter Amanda went upstairs to have the phone call in private. Later she told us that John Edward kept talking to her about a woman who'd lost a leg. When she said it, Patsy's sister Joan exclaimed, "It's Mom!" Their mother had died when Patsy was twelve. Now her sister told her for the first time that right before their mother had died in the hospital, doctors had amputated her leg. It hadn't saved her life. The leg had been sewn back for the funeral, and Joan had never told Patsy. John Edward also said that Eddie, the son who died most recently, wanted to talk to his sister. Patsy put Amanda on the phone. Eddie spoke to Amanda through John Edward. I don't know what was said on the other end of the line, but when Amanda came down she was crying. It was intense, and I knew Patsy's yearning for her children would never be satisfied, but I also knew she was deeply moved.

Dean and I were supposed to have readings too, but John Edward was running out of time. We decided that he would do readings for me and Dean at the same time. We picked up two extensions in Joan's master bedroom, but as soon as we started talking, Dean's people dominated our reading. John Edward doesn't control who comes in, and it was Dean's family who came through, clear as day. His father said something about a truck: his truck was Dean's dad's prized possession. And as for his mother, John Edward said, "She says that you'll know what this means: you took a furniture set of hers." It was true—Dean had his mother's bedroom set. Then John Edward said, "Your mother is saying that she was just with you. She wants you to know she just saw you. At a powwow. I see Indians, tepees, an Indian headdress. Someone vomited. You guys were just there."

I said, "Oh my God, Dean. That woman, that place, the petrified wood, the tepees!" There had been tepees in the desert around the souvenir shop at Stewart's Petrified Wood, where we'd met the woman who struck me as looking exactly as Dean's mother would have looked if she were still alive. And Stella had had a stomach flu the same day. She had vomited in the RV. Everything fit with John Edward's vision. It was mind-blowing. I stared at Dean in amazement. He said, "Oh, wow, that's cool," but (not for the first time) he wasn't as worked up as I was. I don't know if he bought it. It's hard for him to go there. I knew the woman who'd looked like Dean's mother wasn't her, but I still believed that in some way she had come through to see us. It was a huge moment for me. Not so for Dean. I've never heard him tell the story and I'm pretty sure he hasn't thought about it since.

After Dean's parents had their piece, I was waiting, hoping to hear from my father or Nanny or my old friend Jeremy, who passed when I was almost thirty. Then John Edward said, "There's a person here. The person wants to reach out to someone through you, Tori. The person wants to reach out to someone whose name starts with the letter *R*."

I said, "Randy?" Was it my father, trying to reach out to my brother through me?

But John Edward said, "No, no. Richmond?"

I don't know a Richmond. I said, "Randall?" still hoping for Randy.

Then John Edward said, "No. This is really weird, Tori. I have no idea what this means, but I keep getting a picture of Farrah Fawcett."

I said, "Are you sure? I mean, I've lost some important people. Nanny . . ."

He said, "No, it's Farrah. Farrah Fawcett's coming through."

I said, "Well, maybe my dad's there? Behind the hair? Or a young guy named Jeremy?"

John Edward said, "Nope, I'm still getting Farrah Fawcett. Does that make sense?"

I said, "Well, we were neighbors . . ."

John Edward said, "And your father did *Charlie's Angels*."

"True."

John Edward said, "Yeah, it's definitely Farrah."

"That's bizarre," I said. I couldn't imagine why Farrah would want to talk to me. I mean, I knew Farrah. She lived next door to me. She worked on my father's show. We had commiserated one time about bad ex-boyfriends. And it's true that she was dead and was therefore qualified to contact me through an other world specialist. But never in a million years would I have expected Farrah Fawcett to show up at my psychic reading.

John Edward said, "You think it's bizarre for you? Think how bizarre it is for the medium. I've only had a celebrity come through once before and it was royalty."

I laughed.

Dean said, "Farrah was royalty to me in my teenage years."

So Farrah Fawcett hijacked my reading. She told John Edward that she lived near me, which was true. She wanted me to tell her family that she was okay and that she was with her mom. And she wanted to get in touch with her son Redmond. Not my brother Randy. The person whose name started with the letter R was her son Redmond. She kept saying, "Tell him to remember Hawaii and Daffy Duck."

That was the end of it. John Edward hung up and I reflected on the message I had received from beyond. What was I supposed to do with Farrah's request? Call Ryan O'Neal and tell him that Farrah was okay? Contact Redmond in his court-ordered residential rehab program to tell him about Hawaii and Daffy Duck?

I believe in communication from beyond. When Liam says, "There was a monster in my room," Dean tells him, "Oh, I sent him in to make you laugh." But I'm like, "What did the monster look like and where was he standing? What did he tell you?" I couldn't help wondering if it was true. What if Farrah did jump in because it was the only opportunity she had, and I'm the asshole who doesn't reach out to her family? If I saw Redmond and mentioned Daffy Duck, would that turn out to be his childhood nickname? I was dying to find out. But Farrah had chosen her recipient badly. Seriously, I couldn't call Redmond. Me, of all people, selected by a dead person to reach out and give a message? As if I would call someone I don't know, much less call them to give them a message from their dead mother about Daffy Duck. Didn't Farrah know how nonconfrontational I was? Could I ask John Edward to tell her that?

I never called Redmond, of course. It's unresolved and it still kind of haunts me. I should call him. I really should. Shoot.

John Edward wasn't the only surprise we had planned for Patsy. Though we'd only just arrived at her sister's place, the reality was that, unbeknownst to Patsy, we'd actually come to town a day earlier and gone straight to Patsy's house. We had some work to do there.

The whole idea started with a new mattress. I knew Patsy liked our Sleep Number mattress at home. Patsy had always said that her mattress killed her back, and if we got sick of our bed, she'd gladly take it. So when I was still back in L.A., I reached out to Sleep Number. When I told them about Patsy, how she'd just had surgery, and how much she loved our mattress, they agreed to give her a Sleep Number of her own (and no, I didn't get paid to mention them here. Or anyone else for that matter).

Then I started thinking bigger. Patsy's house was new, but she'd gotten it around the time that Eddie died and she'd been working for us almost the whole time since she'd moved in. She'd never had a chance to decorate it, and even now that she was home, she'd been too ill and depressed. I wanted to do something to make her house more of a home. Patsy always said she liked my style. Maybe along with the mattress I'd redo her bedroom. I knew she'd be in there a lot while she was recovering. I asked her daughter Amanda for pictures of the house to see what we could plan.

When I got the photos, I saw that Patsy's bedroom was newly painted, but there were other parts of the house that could use a face-lift. We arrived in Waleska, got the house keys from her sister, and in twenty-four hours, with my friend James's help, we did everything we could to brighten the place up. Our budget was small, so we started by painting everything: we knew we could do that on a shoestring. Patsy loves red, so we did an accent wall in her kitchen. And I knew she'd always wanted a red front door, but people told her she was crazy and shouldn't do it. So we took care of that too. We added new pieces from Pier 1. We framed pictures of her family and hung them on the wall. We found pictures of our kids in a closet and hung them up too. After a day of work, we saw Patsy, talked to John Edward, and told her, "You can't go back to your house today. Sleep at Joan's tonight." She squinted her eyes and said, "I know you're up to something."

The next morning we walked with Patsy over to her house. The whole house was different, there was a lot to absorb, but Patsy's eyes went straight to a picture of Eddie that we'd put up on the wall. She walked over to the picture and said, "Oh, Eddie. He loved this house. He was so excited for me to move in. I always thought he would stay here." Then she just started weeping. Getting her health back, moving on with her life, fixing up her house—I think all of it meant saying good-bye to Eddie, letting him go. Patsy spent a while there, blind to the changes that were all around her, taking the time she needed to mourn Eddie in that moment.

When she was ready, Patsy walked through the whole house with me. I could see that she loved it. She turned to me and said, "Thank you, I don't know what to say."

I said, "You don't need to thank us. I just want you to be happy."

That night all the friends flew home and left us to drive home alone. Dean, the kids, and I stayed an extra night with Patsy. I wanted to cook dinner for her, but we all love her catfish, so she instructed me and I made it for us all. Patsy, her son Chad, Dean, Liam, Stella, and I all had dinner together at her new dining room table. Patsy took only the tiny servings that her surgery would allow. Over the course of our visit she had her real babies and her adopted babies together, and she was on her way to health. It felt right.

Patsy was healing, but as she was rebuilding her life, unbeknownst to me, the life of another beloved family member was coming to an end.

Lost and Found

Toward the end of October my friend Marcel got a call from my mother's assistant on his cell phone. For reasons nobody can remember anymore, Marcel has my old cell phone number from six years ago. I know that at some point my mother had my correct phone number and Dean's, but it shows how out of touch we were that this time her assistant called Marcel's phone. The message she left said that my mother had family news, not about her or Randy, and to please call. I instantly thought, *Something's happened to Uncle Danny.*

The children had visited their grandmother, and it had gone well, but that hadn't yet changed anything between me and my mother. We weren't exactly what anyone would call chatty. Now, in my typical, nonconfrontational way, I emailed my mother's assistant saying, "My friend Marcel said that he got a message from you. I wanted to check in and see if it was you, if it was legit." I added that I couldn't call right then because I was at a loud party. In fact, the Guncles were over for dinner. It wasn't exactly a party, but I was too chicken to pick up the phone.

The assistant responded, "Sorry to disrupt your party. It was me, that was the only number we had on file for you. You can reach your mother on her cell."

We hadn't talked in a long time. I was nervous to call. I'm not proud of being scared to call, but that's the truth. So instead I wrote back, "With two children under three, life is all about disruptions. Did something happen to Uncle Danny?"

Later one of the Guncles would say, "You managed to successfully avoid talking to your mother again. Nicely done." Being nonconfrontational was my habit, but I wasn't trying to make a point or take a stance. This wasn't about me and my mother and our relationship, such as it was. It was about Uncle Danny.

A reply popped up from my mother's assistant. She answered, "Well, your mother didn't want to tell you over email, but your uncle Danny passed yesterday and we wanted you to know."

I stood there in the kitchen, processing the email I'd just received. The Guncles were there with me; Dean was on his way to the airport for a motorcycle race in Vegas. Scout said, "Are you okay?"

I said, "I feel nothing. I should feel something, but I don't."

Bill said, "People deal with things in different ways."

Dean canceled his trip and came right back home. In the kitchen he hugged me and I started to cry, but I tried to stop myself. He said, "What are you doing?"

I said, "It's not all right to cry. It's a sign of weakness. Crying and being comforted makes this about me. People shouldn't feel sorry for me." I felt like I didn't deserve sympathy or attention, maybe because I'm not used to it. I've spent my whole life getting attention, but none of it *personal* attention, none of it attention to my feelings. So I'm not used to that, or I crave it, or I'm all mixed up about it. But Dean told me to let go, and then, in the kitchen with Dean, I let myself cry. Soon I was bawling. Dean said, "This is good. It's okay. You loved him."

My father died before my children were born. It was the order of things and I try not to dwell on it. But after he was gone, Uncle Danny was the closest I could get to my father. Sharing the kids with him was a little like having my dad see them. When Stella turned one, Uncle Danny came to visit. He stayed with us and experienced day-to-day life with the kids. That was the last time we saw him, and it had been a really sweet visit, a memorable good-bye, though I didn't know it at the time.

The feeling that Uncle Danny and I had said good-bye on a nice note was a change for me. When I lost my father, when I lost Nanny, who raised me, even when I lost my beloved dog Mimi La Rue, I felt guilt and regret for not having spent the time I wanted with them at the end of their lives. But I felt no regret about the relationship I had with Uncle Danny. I emailed him all the time. I kept him in my children's lives. We'd had a great visit four months earlier. This time, for once, there was no internal conflict—just grief.

A chapter of my life was over. Uncle Danny had been a parent to me. In a way he was like my dad, his brother; he looked just like him, but he was a different kind of father. He filled in gaps that my father left. My father never asked me questions about my personal life. We had a loving but unemotional relationship that mostly came down to chatting about the dogs. Uncle Danny, on the other hand, actually asked about my thoughts and feelings. Back when I was in my twenties and he'd come to town to visit, he'd say, "When are you going to get married? When are you going to have babies?" When he was visiting for Stella's first birthday, at some point he stared at me, giggling, beaming, and shaking his head. He said, "I just can't believe it. You're a hands-on mom. I can't believe it." I'd never had anyone show that they were proud of me like that.

Now Uncle Danny was gone. I would never again have someone paternal watch over me with pride. That period of my life was over. Nobody was taking care of me. I'd become the emotional matriarch of my family. From now on it would be me taking care of my children, looking down and being proud of them. It was a moment of sadness and a moment of closure.

My younger brother Randy and I, who had always been best friends, hadn't talked for a long time. In our twenties we were inseparable. We had sushi lunches three days a week. We shopped together. I picked out his whole wardrobe at Miu Miu. We spent every weekend together. On Friday nights we'd meet at my apartment with friends and all go out to dinner or a bar. Randy was the one I'd call—before Jenny or Mehran—to give him the blow-by-blow if I went on a date with a new guy. He'd analyze every detail with me. He was my straight Mehran.

Randy stayed neutral while my mom and I were battling it out, first in and around my first wedding and later in the press. I wanted him to take my side. He had always been my best ally. We grew up together. He knew what I was going through, better than anyone else. Amid the public drama, Randy and I had fallen into silence. I had missed Randy, but I couldn't bring myself to pick up the phone. Neither of us did. Once in a while we'd text or email on birthdays or Christmas, but we'd lost our connection.

When Uncle Danny died, Randy wrote me an email. It was the first I'd heard from him in a long time. He said that he knew how much Uncle Danny meant to me and how hard it was for me to lose him. He said that it was so lovely that my kids and I spent time with Uncle Danny. And then he said something like, "It's nice to see that in spite of everything you have become the mother that you always wanted to be." I don't remember the exact words, but I knew it was his way of saying that he supported me, that he always had, that he knew how I'd struggled, and that he respected the mother I'd become. I knew what had gone wrong between us, but I hadn't known what I needed from him to fix it. Now, to my surprise, here it was: all I needed was to have my brother back—as the person who knew me and my past so well, and just as himself. I emailed him back to thank him and to share our sadness.

Uncle Danny's funeral was scheduled for a Friday in Novato, California, where he had lived. It was just after Halloween, and Liam and Stella had been at some parties where crowds of fuzzy, variously costumed kids were coughing all over each other. Since then both kids had been sick with sniffles, coughs, and mild fevers. I myself had a little cough and thought I might be coming down with a cold. Then on Wednesday night, two days before we were scheduled to leave for the funeral, my stomach pain started up again. It hit me hard. I was up all night with a heating pad, feeling achy and uncomfortable.

My first stop in search of a remedy was a holistic doctor. Dean calls her my voodoo doctor, but Jenny had gone to this woman for chronic fatigue with great results. I was impressed. Meanwhile, the regular doctors had never convincingly diagnosed my stomach issues beyond suggesting it might be stress. Maybe this holistic doctor would be able to see a bigger picture.

The first thing the holistic doctor did was test me for the H1N1 virus. She said she was testing all her patients. She handed me a vial to hold in one hand. Then she took my other hand, squeezed my pinkie and thumb together, and tried to pull them apart. If I couldn't keep them together, I had H1N1. She could test for any illness that way! Who needs modern science? Anyway, she said I tested negative for H1N1, but that I had something called parvovirus. I thought only dogs could get parvo, but she told me this was different. "Oh, okay," I said. I took her word for it. Anyone who could diagnose disease via finger muscle testing had to know what she was talking about. At least I didn't have worms. Or ear mites. Now I knew what ailed me. Parvo. She loaded me up with a bag full of herbal supplements and a slumber spray. The total bill for the visit, including the treatments, was nine hundred dollars. Boy, I should have gone to a vet. It would have been cheaper.

On Thursday night I made my shepherd's pie from scratch to take my mind off feeling sick. I was on the living room couch tweeting about how much I love making shepherd's pie when Dean came home. I told him my stomach was killing me. It was so bad, I thought I might have to go back to the hospital, but we couldn't decide what to do. We were supposed to fly to Uncle Danny's funeral at five thirty the next morning. If I spent all night in the emergency room, how would I make it to San Francisco? But if I didn't get medicine for the pain, I wasn't sure I'd survive the flight. Finally, at ten thirty I couldn't take it anymore. We called the Guncles to take care of the kids. As soon as they arrived, we went to a nearby hospital.

By the time they checked me into the ER, I was achy and coughing, with a sore throat and my stomach problem again. They swabbed me for the flu, and even I could see that it was starting to look a lot like the flu. But as they stuck the swab up my nose, I was deliriously saying, "No, it's parvo. It's just parvo. Can you check me for parvo?"

By dawn on Friday all my symptoms had progressed. My stomach pains were dwarfed by what now looked to be a full-blown flu. Except that it was worse than any flu I had ever experienced. I felt like there were golf balls in my throat. It was hard to catch my breath. I clearly wasn't going to make it to Uncle Danny's funeral.

Before I'd gotten sick, I'd been in touch with my mother and my brother about the funeral. My mother wasn't able to attend, but Randy and I both planned to go. We emailed back and forth to make plans, but I also sent him pictures of Liam and Stella. When he got the picture of Liam, he wrote, "He looks like me when I was little; he looks big." It was a reminder of how much time had passed since Randy had seen Liam. I knew Randy and I both wanted to rebuild our relationship. I'm so bad at confrontation, and I knew that seeing Randy at Uncle Danny's funeral would mean that we would talk about what had (and hadn't) gone on between us. Randy wasn't the type to sweep matters under the rug. But this was a confrontation that felt right. We were going to support Uncle Danny, and it would have been the right time to reconnect.

The first day in the local hospital, Dean was in touch with Randy to tell him that I wasn't going to make it to the funeral after all. That evening, when Dean was out getting a bite to eat, my phone rang. I was kind of delirious, but I crawled with my IV over to the table and picked up the phone. It was Randy, calling from L.A. He'd just gotten home from the funeral. He said, "Tor? It's Rand." I hadn't talked to him since Liam was an infant.

Randy and I spoke on the phone for an hour. He talked me through the funeral, telling me who was there and how they remembered Uncle Danny. It was a military funeral with a gun salute. People got up and told stories about how Uncle Danny was a selfless person who had changed their lives. He told me that our cousin Butch, Uncle Danny's son, had the old metal camping plates Danny had used when he was in the army, in World War II. Butch had given Randy three of them, one for him, one for me, and one for my mother.

At the end of the conversation Randy and I didn't make plans to get together. We were treading carefully. It had been a long time. Randy just said, "I'll let you go so you can get some rest."

I said "I love you" to him.

He said, "I love you too."

I was so out of it for most of that day—a day I planned to devote to the memory of my uncle—that it passed in a blur, except for when the doctor came in to say, "Well, they checked the flu swab. You don't have the flu. You might have a cold."

When he breezed out, I looked at Dean. "Was he just mean to me?" A cold! I was dying and he didn't believe me. The doctor had never listened to my chest, looked at my ears, or checked my throat. Did he think I was some nutty celebrity trying to score pain meds? I felt like I was suffocating!

Dean went out to find the doctor and ask him to examine me. A while later they came back together. The doctor listened to my chest. He said, "You have a bit of a wheeze." He ordered an in-room treatment for me and left again. That doctor definitely thought I was being a big baby. I definitely thought he was being a big jerk.

Soon the nurse in charge came in to administer the breathing treatment. She asked how I was and I told her my symptoms. She took one look at me and said, "You have H1N1. You're getting worse. I'm calling the doctor. There are tons of false negatives on the test we do here. The doctor needs to do another test and send it to the lab."

I said, "Are you sure? I think it's parvo."

She said, "Isn't that a canine thing?"

Could I really have the swine flu? I was horrified. Swine flu was still a new phenomenon. The only news reports about it were describing a killer virus, the Big One that was going to take us all down. I didn't know anyone who had contracted it yet, at least anyone who was admitting it. If they got wind of my diagnosis, the press would have a field day: they already mocked me for being thin and being a bad actress. Would they add this to the checklist? First I had a horse face; now I had the pig flu.

I texted Jenny ASAP about my potential diagnosis, feeling dirty and embarrassed. She was calm, just saying, "Don't worry, I know plenty of people who have it. You'll be okay." Was it me, or did she sound *too* calm? Did I hear tears behind that text? Was she convincing me . . . or was she convincing herself? I thought of poor Jenny, rushing to put together a photo album of all our best moments together so she'd have something to share with her kids when I was gone. I envisioned her sitting on the couch with all three of her children, flipping through the pages with tears in her eyes. "Aunt Tori was super funny, one of a kind," she'd tell them . . .

Suddenly a flurry of activity shook me out of my daydream. Three nurses in full protective gear came into the room. They drew the curtains closed around my bed. They put a warning sign on the door and (I imagined) yellow police tape out front. The room was sealed. I was in isolation lockdown. Now every single nurse or orderly who came into the room was covered from head to toe, like in *E.T.* when they're examining the potentially toxic alien. I was an extraterrestrial. Or *The Boy in the Plastic*

Bubble (my father's movie). Poor Dean. They figured he'd already been exposed, so they made him put on a mask whenever he *left* my room.

The doctor followed the nurse's orders and sent a new flu swab off to the lab, but it would take three more days to get the results.

That night the doctor decided to do a CT scan and a spinal tap. My headache was so severe that he wanted to make sure I didn't have meningitis. I mentioned the parvo again, but he clearly thought I was crazy. I decided I probably shouldn't talk about my parvo anymore.

By Sunday morning my headache was so bad that I was crying. The nurses couldn't reach the doctor, who had taken me off pain medication. Apparently the rule was that on the fourth floor, where I was staying, they were not allowed to administer pain medication by IV. IV pain meds were allowed only on the fifth floor. Dean could only take so much of seeing me suffer. He lost it. "This is bullshit," he said.

It was straight out of one of my TV movies, minus the glam hair-and-makeup squad swooping in for touch-ups. Dean the hero unhooked my IV, grabbed his wan, frail wife in his arms, and carried me out of the hospital room. He walked through the halls, into the fourth-floor elevator, and down to the ER. He stood in the middle of the ER, holding me in my paper-thin hospital gown, and demanded, "Can anyone do anything for her? She's in pain and they can't help her on the fourth floor."

The ER nurses looked a little stunned. They listened to Dean, then called up to the fourth floor to check his story. After hanging up, the head nurse said, "Everyone's a little worked up on the fourth floor. Nobody's ever unhooked an IV and removed a patient." Finally they readmitted me to the *fifth* floor, where apparently the pain medication policies were different from the fourth-floor pain medication policies, though we still had the same doctor, who never said anything about Dean's dramatic protest march. In the TV movie he would have been a hunk who tried to steal me from Dean. Oh well.

Two days passed in a blur. On Wednesday, the doctor came in and said, "By the way, we finally got the results back from the flu swab. You tested positive. You do have H1N1, but we have you on Tamiflu. You look better; your chest sounds clear to me. I'm going to release you."

I said, "I really don't feel so good," but he wasn't listening. He dismissed me from the hospital, saying, "You'll feel better in your own bed."

Dean went to get the car while the nurse brought me down to the street. I was white as a ghost. I was hot and sweaty. I couldn't stand up. My headache was through the roof. Something was clearly wrong with me. The nurse said, "If you don't feel well, you'll need to go back in through the ER." I might as well have had parvo, for all that doctor did for me.

Dean said, "Forget it. We're going to Cedars." If this were my death-by-swine-parvo TV movie, I guess this was take two. Dean drove me straight to Cedars-Sinai, the West Hollywood hospital where Liam and Stella were born.

As soon as Cedars found out I was an H1N1-positive patient, I was immediately rushed to an isolation floor. Now it wasn't just my room that was cordoned off for the protection of the public.

It was a whole floor of this hospital, where fellow H1N1 cases suffered in silence behind tightly shut doors like plague victims. After a nurse settled me in a room and left, I thought, *This is the beginning of the end. It's straight out of a movie. Nobody's coming back. They've left us here to die.* Sure, it was an isolation floor now. Clearly it would soon be a makeshift morgue. One of the nurses told me, "This is usually the cardiology floor, but now it's full of people with *it*. I've never seen so many young people on this floor."

An image of a bunch of young, cool people hanging out in the lobby listening to music with IVs in their arms popped into my head. But instead I was stuck in my room entertaining a parade of specialists. The lung specialist and the infectious disease specialist came to see me every day. I'm sure there are many wonderful doctors at the local hospital where we'd gone first, but now the diagnoses came rushing in. I was dehydrated. I had a raging sinus infection that the doctor at the local hospital should have seen on the CT scan. I was having a bad reaction to the spinal tap. They gave me fluids, antibiotics, breathing treatments, and pain medication.

Dean slept on the chair beside me. In the beginning. But after a couple of days I started to improve. And as I started to get better, it turned out that the pain medication I was on made me horny. Dean was happy to take advantage of this new side effect. After the nurses gave me my pain medication, they would leave for the night. Dean would climb into the hospital bed. Dean is six three. The bed was so tiny, he was like a Dr. Seuss character whose feet popped out of one end of the bed or his head stuck out the other.

We had covert sex in that hospital bed. The more I worried that we'd get caught, the more Dean was into it. Dean kept thanking the drug manufacturers and praising their product. And I have to say I think the sex aided my recovery. At home with the kids we always had to find time to have sex. For once there was nothing but time. Yep. I had sex at Cedars. I was a very naughty girl. They may never admit me again.

I spent five days at Cedars after five days at the local hospital. The flu eventually went away, though the headache lingered, but at last it was time for me to go home.

The whole time I was in the hospital and Dean kept me company, the Guncles stayed at our house to take care of the kids. When I finally walked into the house—back home at last—Stella and Liam were upstairs playing in Stella's room. I'd never been away from them for so long. Stella turned, saw me, and gasped, "Mama!" her small mouth forming a little O. Liam heard her, put down a new transformer toy that had appeared while I was gone, and ran into my arms. He was wearing a little skull cardigan that Bill and Scout had bought him at H&M. Maybe they'd had too much fun without me. Liam held my face between his little hands and said, "You sick! You at doctor?" To them ten days is a lifetime. I was afraid they'd forget me or think, *We had a mom once.* Liam suggested that we all go to Mama's bed. The four of us crawled in to watch *Scooby-Doo*.

I was home, depleted and fragile, but home. Uncle Danny was gone and I hadn't really gotten to say good-bye. But something good had come of it. I had thought of Uncle Danny as the last connection I had to my family. My mother and I had a complicated-enough history that at that point I thought whatever relationship we had going forward would be about and through the children. But when Uncle Danny died, my brother came back into the picture. He was a nice, loving person. He didn't have to be perfect. I certainly wasn't. I had my brother. There was no reason for me not to have any family at all. I had chosen that path, chosen to cut off contact, but I could change that decision. I knew Uncle Danny would be happy about me and Randy. His death closed a door, but it opened a new one. A door that had been there all along.

An Imperfect Marriage

People watch *Tori & Dean* and think that we have a perfect marriage. They tell us so—in person or in comments or on Twitter—all the time. It's true that we're a loving couple, but we're human and definitely not perfect.

The show keeps us busy, and we both have side projects. I've taken on several other businesses and projects, and Dean had made his interest in motorcycle racing into more than a hobby. Our careers were in a different place when we met: we were both jockeying hard for auditions. Now work is stable and we've responded to that stability differently. I've become a workaholic and Dean has become a motorcycleholic. That's the simple way of putting it, but it's more complicated than that. For instance, one thing I've noticed is that the more I advance professionally, the more I retreat in my personal life. I apologize to Dean constantly. We both reach for the milk at the same time: "Sorry!" Stella raises her hands for me to pick her up instead of Dean: "Sorry!" I wake up with a headache: "Sorry!" I have to take a phone call: "Sorry!" I said "sorry" too many times this morning: "Sorry!" If somebody bumps into me and nearly knocks me over, I'm the first one to apologize.

All this apologizing drives Dean crazy, and rightfully so. But I can't stop saying it. It's like a tic. I'm not genuinely sorrowful about any of those things, but I compulsively apologize. I want everyone to feel attended to, nobody to be angry, everything to be okay. It's as if my constant apologies can make up for some greater sin that I can't properly address, like I'm saying, "Look, I don't have power! Nothing goes to my head! Don't worry! I promise I'm just a weak little girl!" So my busy mini mogul days, days where I'm making decisions with confidence, are punctuated by this weird self-undermining.

There's no reason for me to act weak for Dean. My success doesn't bother him in the least. The truth is that even if my power did make him uncomfortable, Dean isn't around to witness most of my efforts to build my businesses. What is Dean doing while I'm doing all the nonacting work that doesn't interest him? He's riding motorcycles. Or maintaining motorcycles. Or buying motorcycle gear. Or talking about motorcycles with his friends who race motorcycles.

The motorcycle issue is my fault. I started it. Or at least revved an engine that was idling. Dean rode motorcycles in his first marriage; his wife wasn't cool with it; he quit. Then I came along. I wanted to be different. I wanted to be all-accepting. I wanted to make him happy. So for Father's Day I rented him a motorcycle.

Nice move, Tori. I did this knowing full well how swept up Dean gets in his hobbies. I'd already almost lost him to scuba diving. And I knew how dangerous motorcycles are. So why did I get him started? Am I an enabler? Was I sabotaging us? I should have known better.

I never asked Dean to stop, but when he saw how upset I was by the motorcycles, he quit. He had all of his motorcycles taken away to be sold. But then we had a conversation in which I told him I didn't want him to sell them. I wanted him to finish what he started. I just wanted him to make more time for us. And to be safe. He had them brought back.

Dean knows the danger, and he does everything he can to ride safely, but how can you be safe and responsible when you're doing something that's fundamentally dangerous? Dean is careful, but part of him just believes that when your time is up, your time is up. When he brought the bikes back, he said, "I strongly believe I'm going to live to a ripe old age. I just know it. My grandma lived to ninety-nine. She was healthy as a horse. She walked to the racetrack every day and had her wee nip of brandy. I'm not going to stop racing or scuba diving. What a wasted life if I got hit by a bus and found myself sitting up in heaven having to admit that I didn't do anything because I was afraid I'd die. I want to live my life."

This is the exact opposite of how I think. I live life as though death is waiting just around the corner, and therefore I should do everything humanly possible to protect myself while turning that corner, including, but not limited to, wearing mystical bracelets, performing superstitious rituals, consulting spiritual guides,

enduring voodoo cleansings, sweating, crying, shaking, convuls-
ing in fear, and, sometimes, just turning around and going in the
opposite direction, regardless of whether I can still get where I
need to go.

Dean likes the camaraderie of the pit, but he says that when
he's out on the track, it's an individual sport. He says, "In the
middle of a race I'm a rock star. I'm Ben Spies. I'm Mat Mladin.
I'm Valentino Rossi."

To which I say, "The name Valentino rings a bell."

And he also says that when he's racing there is nothing in his
head. He is free from the weight of the world. He feels like he is
flying.

Yeah, maybe this is part of the problem. My husband loves to
feel like he's flying? To me that's like saying you love to feel like
you're getting a tooth pulled. But okay. Different strokes and all
that. Dean gets from racing some of what I get out of running my
businesses—the feeling of power and knowing exactly what you
want and need to do. And I see that it also gets him out of his
head, which I could certainly use. But when he says he feels like
he's escaping the weight of the world, I can't help feeling like that
world that he's escaping is *us,* his family.

If Dean has a day off, he's off to the racetrack. I crave more time
with Liam and Stella. If I have a day off, it is automatically theirs.
There are things I miss about being single. Before I had kids, I
loved to get into bed at three in the afternoon and spend hours
watching mindless chick flicks, stupid movies, reality TV, and *E!
True Hollywood Stories.* Now I can't imagine doing that. I can't

imagine what a day to myself would be like. I'm not even sure I would be able to relax and enjoy it.

But maybe that's my problem, not his. Dean has taken on producing jobs, but he still finds a way to race and scuba dive, and he says that if he didn't, he'd go insane. He says it's not a happy life if you work hard but can't enjoy the fruits of your labor.

Just because I'm a workaholic doesn't mean Dean has to be one too. It's not a good thing to be. I'm the one who feels a need for a certain kind of life. Dean would choose a simpler way of being. Hadn't he been trying to tell me that all summer? My workaholic life was making me sick. *He* is the one who has found a healthier balance. Except that motorcycles are so dangerous, so that isn't healthy. And then I'm back in the cycle of resentment.

Dean does spend time with the children. He is a devoted father. But he also gives time to his other interests. He finds enough free time to do both. He wishes I could do the same—and wishes I were less fearful. When I rented him the motorcycle for Father's Day, he wanted nothing more than for me to hop on the back.

Clearly I need to make my peace with Dean's motorcycle habit, but I haven't done it. Instead, my fear has turned to anger. I decided that if he died riding a motorcycle, I would not mourn him. He knows I don't like it. He knows it's dangerous. Yet he continues to do it. I refuse to mourn a death I tried to prevent. Jenny says, "It doesn't matter: you'd be destroyed if you lost Dean. It doesn't matter how." Of course. I mean, we all know that I'd grieve, but I don't know how else to make my point.

So I say, "Nope, I will not grieve."

Dean knows not to take me at face value. But he always protests anyway. He says, "You've always said you couldn't picture life without me. Now you're saying you won't grieve for me if I die?"

I say, "I've said my piece." The first time I said it, I threw my head back, turned on my heel, and made my exit. Now that I've said it so many times, I don't bother with the dramatic flourishes anymore.

Jenny insists that if her husband wanted to ride motorcycles, she would just say no. She would demand that he give it up, and if I know Norm, he would. For better or worse, I refuse to make rules for Dean. Instead I just roil in resentment. He's off doing his life-threatening gear-head man hobby while I'm working my ass off.

Any work-life balance can work in a relationship if both people accept it, but I go back and forth. I'm a workaholic. I want to control everything. I want to do it all, but then I resent it. I get mad about working so hard when Dean doesn't have to. There was a moment in *Tori & Dean* that showed me working like a dog while Dean went to the motorcycle track to ride. He knows that he's hanging out while I'm working and he admits to the camera, "I'm a douche bag." When I saw that moment on tape, the resentment drained right out of me. Having him acknowledge the difference in our daily lives meant everything to me. Ah, the therapeutic benefits of reality television.

Our conflict around the motorcycles symbolized some other issues that were coming up—the chronic imbalance of work, time, and gender that come into play in most marriages. I couldn't help wondering if part of what appealed to Dean about the motor- cycles was the power he has in that world. It's not just the tough leather duds. Among his motorcycle buddies, Dean is the big shot. He's the star.

Recently Dean went to New York by himself to promote a movie that he was in. The morning after he got home, he told me that he was going to a motorcycle and car event that night, with his motorcycle buddy Santiago. I was taken aback. He'd just gotten home the night before. I said, "Oh. I thought we could all spend time together." Dean relented immediately. No big deal. He wouldn't go. But I stayed mad all morning. Why did he want to go? Why didn't he want to be with us, with me? I couldn't understand why he wanted to go to the motorcycle event without us. It seemed like a big deal. It was meaningful. Dean didn't see the complexity of the matter.

He said, "I was invited. They have retro cars."

But I said, "You were going to take Santiago instead of me. When I was married to Charlie, I used to take Mehran to events." Now I was doing something I'd told Dean not to do—jump- ing to compare our relationship to mine with my ex. But in this case I thought he was behaving like I did when I was trying to escape.

Dean said, "You feel like it's your relationship with Charlie because of one night?" I reminded him that when we first got together, we never wanted to be apart, not for a minute. For me, losing that was more significant than the changes to our sex life which were so frustrating to Dean. He kept saying, "But it's motorcycles and cars. You don't like that stuff. If you were taking Mehran to a jewelry event, I wouldn't care."

I said, "But I'd want to take you. We're soul mates. We want to be by each other's side. I like that we do everything together. I don't want us to diverge."

Then we got to what I thought was the heart of the matter. He said, "You don't like to go to events anymore because you're tired of it, but it's still kind of new for me. I get invitations and it's pretty cool." It's true that before Dean and I had kids, we went to a lot of events. We went to at least one every week. Restaurant openings, store launches, art gallery events, screenings, magazine parties, L.A. Fashion Week. It was fun. But I'd had enough, and I wanted him to feel the same way. As far as I was concerned, once we had kids, we moved on to the next chapter of our lives, but Dean never really had that chapter. He still wanted to enjoy the attention and perks of fame.

In some ways our lives are moving faster than Dean would like. He often says, "Remember when . . ." And when he says that, what I hear is "Remember when you were fun." Before we got so busy with work and I got pregnant, I stayed out late, drank, had sex on demand. Now he says, "I miss us alone." We'd been married for only two months when I got pregnant with Liam.

For me, the us that was me and Dean evolved into the us that is me, Dean, Liam, and Stella. I didn't miss the us we used to be. Whatever had changed, whatever we'd lost, that was part of being a grown-up. Life was give-and-take. What we'd gotten in return, as parents, was much bigger than whatever we'd sacrificed.

I think some people miss the attention that they got from their spouses before the kids came along. And the freedom. I don't miss it. If I take time for myself, I just feel guilty anyway. I used to get pedicures every week, but the idea of my kids sitting at home with a sitter while someone fiddles with my feet just seems out of whack. When I do drag myself to a pedicure, I spend the whole time on my BlackBerry, trying to be productive.

I understood that Dean didn't get to experience the celebrity whirlwind for all the years I did. I didn't want to take that away from him, but I also didn't want that to be our lives. I thought back to a few weeks earlier when we'd been invited to a premiere. Dean RSVP'd yes right away. When he told me we were going, I said, "You said yes? I hate premieres."

Dean said, "You do?"

Yeah, I do. I used to like premieres. Once, when I went to *Interview with a Vampire,* I wore a cropped angora midriff top and leather pants. I brought Jenny as my date. We were waiting on the press line when Jenny got body-slammed. She went down, sprawled across the red carpet. She was lying there, horrified, when an arm came out of nowhere. A deep voice said, "I'm so sorry." Jenny looked up and saw that it was Brad Pitt. She said, "It's okay." He helped her to her feet. To this day, when Jenny gets sentimental about the good old days she says, "Remember when Brad Pitt almost killed me on a press line?" and sighs dreamily.

But those days were over for me. I'd had that experience and I was done. Now Dean wanted to go to premieres all over again. Why would I want to get all dressed up to watch a movie when we could put on sweats and watch it in our den on a Saturday night?

I said, "We went to *Star Trek.* Wasn't that enough?"

Dean and I have been together for four years, and in that time he has become a household name through our show and in motorcycle circles. Our social life used to be powered by my celebrity, but things are changing. When he was in New York, Dean was on the *Today* show. He said, "The publicity trip was about my movie. The press was following me. I felt important." Another time he was invited to a gifting suite here in L.A. He went without me, and afterward he said, "It was cool. They invited me. They gave me things. Who doesn't like that?" I liked to hear that he was having fun. But to me he was always important. And he's already a successful actor in his own right, with or without the perks.

Dean and I met as equals, working on the same movie, but at the time I was careful to talk about the imbalance in our careers and celebrity. I'd been in Hollywood for a long time. I had celebrity through my family, through my shows, and, well, just a disproportionate share of celebrity in general. Dean got it. He knew what I was worried about. It's hard for actor couples when one gets more attention. It's not a great feeling, and it can be the downfall in relationships between people in our business. The relationships often fail. Dean said he was content to take the back seat. He said, "I've been doing this for a long time. You've been famous forever and you've worked hard for it. That's the way it's going to be. I'm not going to be jealous of my wife." I know he still feels that way about the differences in our careers. This wasn't about competing with me on any level. But midlife, success, love, desires, attention—complex emotions circle around us, and no matter how much we talk things through, we can surprise ourselves. For some reason motorcycles mean so much to Dean that he continues to ride them in spite of the danger and my reaction. I don't understand what that reason is; I might never understand it, but I know it is very real and important to him.

We didn't really resolve our fight about the motorcycle event except that Dean didn't attend the event that night. Then just after dinner Santiago came over to drop off Dean's truck. Instead of saying, "Thanks for returning the truck," Dean sat down with Santiago and they talked for two hours. The kids were ready for bed and Dean wasn't there to say good night. We'd *just* had a fight about this. The whole point of Dean staying home from the event was that he spend time with the family! The whole point was that I wanted him to *want* to be with his family. He hadn't gone out, but he might as well have.

As Dean and Santiago shot the breeze, I was upstairs seething. But instead of going down to Dean and telling him what I needed, I sent Liam to do my dirty work. I said, "Tell Daddy to stop talking."

Liam dutifully trotted to the top of the staircase and yelled, "Hey, guys, shut up. Stop talking. Daddy come!" Liam came back to me all proud and we high-fived. Great, Tori, way to use your child to communicate with your husband.

Why was Dean doing this? He knew my issues. I'd been very clear. There had to be anger that he wasn't expressing. He still wanted what he wanted. And maybe he didn't want to feel like I was controlling him and his time. I didn't say anything; I waited and watched. The next night he asked to take me out on a date, wherever I wanted to go. He wanted to make me happy. He wanted to be with me. But he wanted to do it on his terms.

During the fight about the motorcycle event, when I told Dean I was worried about our relationship, he said, "We have a great relationship. When I was in New York everyone was talking about what a great relationship we have."

I said, "Yeah, I was on Twitter missing you." That was real. I did miss him. But people say we have a perfect relationship, we hear it, and we buy into it. When I watch the show I think that we're perfect too. It doesn't show me nagging. It doesn't show him nitpicking at how I do things. We forget that there's a difference between image and reality.

Dean and I are in a solid, committed relationship, but it's not always perfect. Things change. Relationships have ebbs and flows. The tabloids had it all wrong. We weren't in a loveless marriage. Dean never said any of those horrible things his former friend claimed were true. But that autumn was hard. We were in ebb.

Liam's Word

I wasn't just a workaholic. I was a momaholic. Part of it was my preexisting perfectionism, and part of it was wanting to prove that I was just another normal mom.

Over the summer Liam was still going to school. One of the moms came up to me and invited me to a playdate in Pasadena. It sounded great, but we were staying at the beach, which is over an hour from Pasadena, so I said we couldn't come. The mom said, "Of course not. You don't go to anything."

I think of myself as an involved mother, and the implication that I wasn't irked me. Here I was being realistic about our chances of coming to one playdate, and I was being told that this was my MO by the same mom who didn't like that I was going to drive Liam the two blocks home from a playdate with poop in his diaper.

I'm a perfectionist, which means I try to do everything to the fullest, to a fault. As Liam began preschool, I started bringing Stella to the same Mommy & Me class that I did with Liam the year before. One day I was in Stella's classroom and noticed a sheet in the back of the room with a pen hanging from it. It was a sign-up sheet, where parents could volunteer to help with holiday celebrations, bringing food or paper goods, doing crafts, and so on. Holiday parties! This was right up my alley. I immediately put my name down next to food for Halloween and Christmas. I would have signed up for Thanksgiving too, but the school hosted the feast for that holiday.

As I was writing, all the other parents floated over to see the sign-up. I glanced up from my sign-up frenzy to see that I was surrounded. I wanted to put my name everywhere, but now they were all watching. One of the moms said, "Oh, you've signed up for all the food through the end of the year." I had? I looked back at the sheet. I had just signed up in two places. It didn't seem like a big deal. The sheet had the rest of the school calendar. She was lucky I hadn't signed up for Valentine's Day, Saint Patrick's Day, Passover, Easter, Leif Erikson Day. I was trying to be polite by only signing up through December! The truth was that I was too much of a control freak to leave any of the holidays in their hands. I knew what that would mean: store-bought food! Cue ominous horror movie music.

The year before, for Liam's toddler class graduation, all the moms were to bring snacks for a celebration. I made little ham and cheese sandwiches and arranged them on the plate in a design. The other snacks included cookies still in the Whole Foods packaging and crudités in a plastic arrangement that had come straight from the grocery store. Moms are busy. Some don't cook. I know such choices are perfectly reasonable. But I am Candy Spelling's daughter. My hostess genes kicked in. I just couldn't let that happen again. Plastic grocery store containers, imagine!

The mom who had noticed my hyperactive sign-ups saw that I was embarrassed at her reaction and said, "I'm just impressed that you'd want to sign up for all that. Go for it." So I left Stella's class having signed up for all the food. Then I went to Liam's class and did the same thing.

The night before Halloween I was up all night making food art for the school. I started by making white and orange worms out of string cheese with pretzel antennae. At first I laid the worms out on a disposable tin tray that was lined with wax paper, but that didn't look good enough. The wax paper had to go. As I started carefully peeling the worms off the tray to start all over again, Dean said, "Only you. Why are you doing this?" He thought I was ridiculous, redoing the whole tray. But I said, "Let me do it! The worms don't look good." I used some food coloring to dye some shredded coconut green and laid it out on the tray as grass. Then I put the worms back on. Now they had a place to crawl and appear wormlike. Perfect. Next I made turkey and cheese sandwiches and cut them with pumpkin-shaped cookie cutters. I lightly brushed them with orange food color and gave them tiny olive eyes. I made English muffin pizzas with ghoulish rubber fingers sticking out. Dean and Scout helped. We had fun with it.

The next morning I brought the platters of food into the school kitchen. The woman who worked in the kitchen saw what I was putting on the counter and said, "Oh my God, this wins!" I thanked her calmly, but when I walked out the door, I did an air pump in the courtyard. I said, "I won! She said I won!"

Dean shook his head. "It's not about winning," he said. No, of course not. I knew that. I loved the process of making the food regardless of how it was received. But the praise also felt good. And I had to admit to myself that there was part of me that wanted to show the other moms that I wasn't what they might assume—the spoiled Hollywood girl who never went on playdates and probably hired a caterer to do food for a preschool party. I was a normal working mom who tried to do it all.

A few months later, for the Christmas party, I went all out again. I made several platters, but my favorite was the chicken nugget snowmen with little hats from eggplant skin, olive eyes, carrot noses, and shaved carrot scarves. Their arms were pretzels. The buttons were green peas. Everything was glued on with cream cheese.

Most of the time it's fun, but sometimes my Martha Stewarting gets out of control and Dean and I clash over my perfectionism. Liam had an "All About Me" day at school. He was supposed to bring in a poster board that showed his family members, his friends, and things he liked. On his "All About Me" day I would go in to spend the day with him at school, bringing along his favorite book, favorite toy, and favorite snack.

For the poster board I went to Michael's, the local craft store, and spent two hundred dollars on stickers. Dean said, "If you're trying to prove that you're a normal mom, let me tell you. That's not normal. That's crazy."

I ignored Dean (buzzkill!) and set about my work. I decided to give the poster the heading "Liam's World." As in "Elmo's World." I had purchased sticker letters in a large font. But as I was spelling out "World," I realized that I only had one of each letter. Once I'd used the *L* for "Liam," there wasn't another for "World." Now the poster said "LIAM'S WORD," with a blank space where the second *L* should be. This was very bad. I was distraught. What could I do? I didn't want to write in an *L*. It wouldn't match. We had to go back to the store. Scout was trying to convince me to make an *L* out of the *T* when Dean walked back into the room. He asked what the fuss was about. I told him I was missing an *L* and had to go back to Michael's. Dean said, "That's ridiculous!" Whoa. I didn't want to challenge Dean. But the *T* made a crappy makeshift *L*. I couldn't stop staring at it.

Scout said, "You know she's going back to the store." But Dean wanted me to be done with it.

I said, "Choose your battles. Maybe you're right, but this is who I am." I put the poster aside until I had a chance to get more letters. But by the time I got back to the craft store, I had decided that "Liam's World" was so last month. He had ditched Elmo for a new superhero obsession. So I trashed the old board and started from scratch. I labored over a new "Super Liam" board. When I was finally done, I emailed his teacher, telling her that I was ready to come in for Liam's "All About Me" day. I told her how guilty I felt; it had taken me so long to get it perfect in the second round. I figured I was the only parent who hadn't made a presentation yet. But she said not to worry, that half the parents hadn't done theirs yet. I signed up right away, so I wouldn't be last. Phew.

I know when Dean tries to curtail my perfectionism he wants

to simplify my life. He sees me stressed out and trying to control every detail and thinks he can help me let go by telling me to let go. Sometimes I wish I could. Being a control freak isn't ideal when you're parenting young children. For school Stella did a project that involved putting stickers on a picture frame. She was piling them one on top of the next, enjoying herself thoroughly. I tried to show her how to distribute them around the frame, but she thought that was lame and went right along sticking them together. Inside I was dying.

It's hard for me to let go, and it's hard for me to just be. I'm constantly in and out of the moment. Helping the kids but thinking about work. Working but missing the kids. No wonder I keep ending up in the hospital.

My perfectionism takes its toll on our lives. It inhibits Dean. This became clear to me when it came time to decorate our Christmas tree. When Christmas came around we bought a living Christmas tree. It's a live tree, with roots still intact, that you "borrow" for Christmas and return afterward to the tree farm. They nurture it over the year, and you get the same tree the next year. I loved the idea that every year when Christmas was over, instead of dumping a sad, dried-out, dying tree, we'd be watching something grow alongside the children.

The kids' homemade ornaments would go on their small individual trees, but for the tree in the family room I selected a specific color scheme that coordinated with the room decor. (Doesn't everyone?) The ornaments—in brown, gold, copper, silver, and cream—were in boxes on the floor next to the tree, ready to be hung. But who had time to hang them?

Christmas was a bustling time in our house. I was still feeling sick, but there were many gifts to be selected, purchased, and nicely wrapped (though not as beautifully as my mom would do it). Our dining room became a gift room as I selected the perfect gifts for our agents, lawyers, business managers, publicist, and all their assistants, and all the assistants' assistants. I bought presents for the people who work on *Tori & Dean,* people at Oxygen, Little Maven, HSN, Simon & Schuster. The more businesses you have, the more people you work with. Then there were our relatives, our friends, and our friends' kids.

I was overwhelmed, and I got it in my head that the one thing I wanted Dean to spearhead was the tree trimming. I texted him a couple of times, saying in my passive way, "would love help with the tree," to which he always responded, "Sure, just let me know, babe." What I didn't say and he didn't get was that I wanted him to just get it done. I was trying to delegate, but apparently even when I made an effort to do it, I wasn't very good at it.

A few days passed, and finally I came in one night and saw that Dean was chilling out, watching some hockey. How relaxing for him! But we had so much to do. It killed me that he was completely oblivious to the holiday to-do list that was expanding daily in my head. I got my jacket and purse, came back into the room all bundled up, and said, "The kids are in the playroom. Can you take over? I'm going out."

He said, "Sure, where are you going?"

I said, "I'm going to CVS to get stocking stuffers for the kids."

He said, "Now? At five thirty on a Sunday night?"

I said, "Well, there's so much to get done before Christmas.

I have to do something." Then I burst out with my real point, telling him how much there was to do and couldn't he just do one little thing—the tree!—while I was out? Dean said he'd been waiting to do the tree with me because I was so controlling that if he went ahead with the decorations, he knew I'd find fault with his work and need to do it all over again.

Now, wait just a minute. We knew I was controlling, but I had never been controlling about the Christmas tree. Well . . . not yet anyway. I wanted to be presumed innocent! Anyway, once I gave him artistic freedom, Dean went in to decorate the tree. Calmer now, I took my jacket off and went into the kitchen to make shepherd's pie and mulled wine for dinner. I had the shepherd's pie halfway into the oven when I remembered that the last time I made shepherd's pie, I ended up going to the hospital at ten thirty that night. I had a nascent shepherd's pie superstition. What if I made this one and ended up in the hospital again? It half crossed my mind to dump the whole pan, but that would be silly. After a moment's hesitation I put it in the oven.

I'm controlling and Dean is an extremist. From the kitchen I heard him shift into work mode. I could hear him instructing Liam, powering through the tree trimming in his über-focused way.

When they were done, I came into the room to see how it looked. Dean and I stood in the doorway together appreciating his handiwork. My boys put together a really beautiful tree. We didn't have a tree topper, so Dean tied three stars together very prettily. He's good at stuff like that. "It looks amazing," I said.

"Are you sure?" he asked. "I know you have a specific way you like things." But it was true. I honestly didn't want to move a single bulb. I had delegated. Dean had helped. It was almost Christmas and maybe we were finding a healthy balance.

But that night I ended up in the hospital with a migraine. Damned shepherd's pie.

The Wootle's on Fire

When all else fails, blame it on an evil eye. That was what I told myself after yet another migraine. I mean, I was sick again. Or I'd never gotten better.

That December night, after decorating the tree, Dean took Liam upstairs for a bath. Stella was asleep, so while the shepherd's pie baked, I sat down and forced myself to read *Martha Stewart Living*. But I couldn't unwind. I felt like I was cheating. A ghostly voice inside my head whispered, "You should be *wooooorking* . . ." I tried to ignore it and keep reading, but I was too weak, powerless to stop myself from doing something. So as I went through the magazine, I started marking potential Christmas presents. Then I pulled out a piece of paper and started making yet another Christmas list. And then I started composing a tweet in my head—about Christmas lists and shopping for colleagues. And then . . .

the headache. I hadn't been sitting for twenty minutes when I felt it coming on.

Maybe my body was protesting the way I'd been treating it. My father was a workaholic and so was I. I was too damned exhausted, and this was my way of forcing myself to take a break that I would never otherwise allow myself. It's no accident that when I was hospitalized the first time, it felt like more of a vacation than my trip to Maui or my summer in Malibu.

Dean thought I was like an addict who hadn't hit rock bottom yet, sneaking off to get a fix of checking Little Maven catalogue shots and approving HSN jewelry samples when no one was looking. I spent all day every day working, being a mom, being a wife, crashing, and doing it all over again.

I was building my life, but I wasn't leaving any space to enjoy it.

Was this really all my fault? Was it stress? That was so . . . middle-aged. I was too young to be suffering from stress, wasn't I? Couldn't it be something a little more original like, oh, an evil eye? I'd once before had an evil eye lifted by a world-renowned voodoo priestess named Mama Lola. And the very next day I'd met Dean. Did Mama Lola really free me from an evil eye, or was it simply the mere belief that she'd cleared me that gave me the confidence to move forward? Answer: who cares? If placebo healing worked on me, then I was all for it.

Then I remembered the red bracelet. When I was newly pregnant with Stella, I met a psychic who told me that people were putting evil eyes on me. As she pulled cards she said, "A woman's put an evil eye on you. I think it could be your husband's ex." I said, "Why would she do that?"

The psychic reminded me that people don't always intentionally put evil eyes on people. That made sense. How often do you hear about people going around saying, "I've got like three evil eyes to put on people tonight. Can we take a rain check on dinner?" She said that evil eyes can just emerge if someone has negative thoughts about you. Mary Jo could have done it without even being aware of it. The psychic gave me a little red bracelet for protection. Don't ask me how this works: it's like electronics to me, wondrous and magical. She told me it was from Israel and blessed it. I faithfully wore it for over two years. Then, this August at the beach in Malibu, I took it off and forgot about it.

August. That was when Dean and I started having fights. In September I went into the hospital with stomach problems. In November it was H1N1, then the relentless headache, and I hadn't felt right since. It was an evil eye, I was sure of it. I'd had nothing but trouble since I took off that bracelet.

That Saturday, when I took the kids to sit on Santa's knee, a bird shat in my hair. Now some people say that that's good luck, although to me it's always sounded like one of those BS things people say when there's no upside, like rained-out weddings. You know what's really good luck? Not getting shat on by a bird. Still, I needed whatever I could get. I would have bought a pigeon and walked around with it superglued to my hair so it could infuse me with regular foul doses of luck if I thought it might help. Between the bird shit and the dead poultry I knew Mama Lola used in her voodoo, my life improvement methodology was all about the foul fowl. I should have kept Milton the pig. He was so uninhibited about his feces. But then I realized: good luck might win me five bucks in a scratch-off game, but it couldn't lift a genuine evil eye. For that I needed to bring in the big guns. This was a job for Mama Lola.

As luck would have it (oh, thank you, bird shit?), Mama Lola was coming to L.A. Through her goddaughter Brandy I asked if she could perform a cleanse on me and we made a date. I did have one special request. During my first cleansing Mama Lola had shocked me by killing a chicken before my eyes. It was rough. I wanted to lift my theoretical evil eye, but I wasn't willing to off another chicken for the cause, so I asked that there please be no slaughtering of live animals during the ritual. Yes, I felt like that annoying friend of a friend at a restaurant who asks, "Do you have any vegan options?" But I was adamant. Brandy said she'd pass on my request to Mama Lola.

The next time I saw Mehran he told me that he'd seen some shows about voodoo. He said that voodoo only really works with the sacrifice of live animals. You need to move the bad energy into something that was living. If you don't, the voodoo doesn't work.

"Why are you doing this to me?" I wailed. "I can't sacrifice a bird. What about my children?"

Mehran sounded shocked. "You want to sacrifice your children?"

"No," I explained. "What kind of lesson would I be teaching them?"

He said, "But you have to lift the evil eye for the sake of your children. So you can stop being sick and be a good mom." He had a point. I decided to worry about the slaughter when the time came.

Mama Lola arrived on a Friday afternoon with Zaar, the reader and spiritual consultant who works with her. Before we started the cleanse, Zaar made the rounds of our house looking for evil spirits. He cleansed all the mirrors and blessed them. I told him to be sure to check the mirror in Stella's room because every night when I walked by it I felt like I caught a glimpse of something creepy out of the corner of my eye. It was an antique standing mirror that I'd purchased back when I was in the money. It stood next to the crib in the corner of Stella's room. Indeed, when Zaar examined it, he found an old spirit lurking there, a spirit with bad energy. Zaar blessed the mirror, which meant that the spirit was supposed to leave, but according to Zaar that stubborn evil spirit was stuck in the mirror. I know, I know. At first it sounded like the Exorcist's version of a shady auto repair shop: "Ooh, this is a bigger problem than we thought it was gonna be. We can't unstick the negative spirit, so we're gonna have to replace the whole spectral transmission." But Zaar was really concerned. He went into the other room to tell Mama Lola. All I heard her say was "Get it out! Get it out!" The mirror had to go.

Mehran turned to me and said, "What are you going to do?"

I said, "Are you kidding? It's got to go." I wasn't about to let some creepy spirit hang out in my daughter's room! So Zaar and Mehran picked up the beautiful, heavy mirror and inched down the front stairs with it.

When they got the mirror down to the front hall, Mehran said, "What are we going to do with it? It's too ghetto to just put it out on the street."

Zaar told me I couldn't give the mirror to anyone and I couldn't sell it. I was supposed to wrap it in a white sheet, smash it, then bury it and plant a gardenia over it. Well, that sounded like a fun weekend-long do-it-yourself project. I asked them to put it out by the side of the house until I got around to it (in some other lifetime).

I knew from my last experience that the first part of the cleanse—the "bad bath"—was the part where the slaughter was supposed to occur. Now the bad bath was upon us. I'd made my request, but the issue still hadn't been resolved. Mama Lola asked if we had the live chicken ready for the sacrifice. I turned to Zaar. "Can it be a worm? From the dirt?"

My producer Megan, who was there because (of course) we were filming the cleanse for *Tori & Dean*, added, "Can it be a hamster? A guinea pig?"

Zaar said, "It needs wings."

Mama Lola said, "It has to be a chicken." It was now seven p.m. on a Friday. The producer left the room to do some research.

When Megan came back she said, "The only live chicken we can find is an actor animal named Liz Taylor. She can be here within an hour, but she has to be returned tomorrow. Um, alive."

I said, "No, this is *real*!" An actor chicken missed the point entirely. Finally I just said that I refused to kill anything, even if it meant the voodoo wouldn't work. We told Mama Lola we couldn't find any live chickens in all of Los Angeles.

Mama Lola, undaunted by my chicken restrictions, began to mix the bad bath that she would use to rid me of the evil spirit. In a large bowl, she combined cornmeal, dried beans, vegetables, and chopped-up yams. She added gin and Florida water, a cologne from the nineteenth century that's still popular in South American and Caribbean cultures. I know: worst gazpacho ever. I stood on newspaper wearing a tank top and underwear while Mama Lola chanted and told me to say that I wanted everything bad to be gone. As she chanted she slashed my clothing into strips. It was very Adrienne Barbeau in *Swamp Thing*.

I wanted to be in the moment, but there were cameras in the room. It was hard not to worry about what I looked like and how the scene would play on our show. I must have looked self-conscious, because my producer Bobby said, "Do you want us to put the cameras down?"

But I said, "No, it's fine. Let's just film it." Having an evil eye cleansed at the same time as I executive-produced a reality show—that must have a place in the Guinness Book of Workaholic Records. Weirdest multitasking ever.

Mama Lola took the mixture. She put it first on my hair, then on my face. It stung my eyes so badly that I couldn't open them, but Mama Lola said, "You're fine, you're fine." Sure, tell that to my ophthalmologist.

Mama Lola poured the mixture all over me. I was soaking wet, smelly, almost naked, and so cold that my teeth were chattering. It was the middle of winter and I had the immune system of a goldfish. Mehran was laughing at me, which pretty much killed the spiritual vibe in the room, if the cameras hadn't already. But Mama Lola wasn't daunted. She was very businesslike about her voodoo.

Then Mama Lola said, "Take it and wipe yourself with it." She indicated that I should scoop a handful of her mixture, then reach in my underwear and wipe. Mehran's jaw dropped. The sound guy coughed and made an odd face. This was a new level of public humiliation, but what could I do? I'd come this far. So in front of Mama Lola, Zaar, Mehran, two cameramen, two producers, and a soundman, I wiped myself with the mixture. Yeesh, it burned so badly. I yelped, "The wootle's on fire! The wootle's on fire!" (Jennie Garth taught me *wootle* back in the *90210* days. Her word. Credit where credit is due.)

I flashed back to when I made the sitcom *So NoTORIous,* based on my life. For one episode we re-created my first cleanse; Whoopi Goldberg played Mama Lola. Now we were filming the real thing, and Mama Lola (on reality TV) was even better than Whoopi Goldberg (on TV) playing Mama Lola (in reality). There was a life lesson in that somewhere, but I was in no condition to parse it. My hooha was burning. But at least no chickens had died. The bad bath was over.

Mama Lola cut off my underwear and tank top (believe me, I wasn't sorry to see them go) in front of everyone (that I *was* sorry about). I wasn't stark naked in front of the crew: she handed me a towel just in time. She put them in a trash bag and beckoned to Zaar and my producer Vidas. She told them to drive at least three miles away and to dispose of my underwear at a crossroads. I thought about Vidas, a happily married man, going home to his wife that night. She'd say, "How was your day, dear?" How would he respond?

I turned to him and said, "Vidas, I'm sorry that after a long day you're driving my soiled underwear three miles from my house to a crossroads."

He said, "Not a problem, T. Not a problem."

During the cleanse Dean was in New York doing publicity for his movie *Santa Baby*. A few days later he was checking on Stella and he noticed the mirror was gone. I sheepishly explained where it was. He said, "You know, I think there's an evil spirit in those lobster dishes you kept from your first marriage." Ha-ha.

Dean was cool with the cleanse—maybe not the mirror trashing (it was a nice mirror!) or the public underwear slashing (he wasn't there to watch!), but the rest of it. He thinks I'm out there with my beliefs, but he likes the idea of Mama Lola because he loves the story that she brought us together after my first cleanse.

A few days later Mama Lola came back to administer the good bath. I knew from before that this was the easy part. The only preparation she asked me to do was to find seven different perfumes. Mehran and I went to CVS to make our selections. It would have been a much shorter trip if I hadn't brought Mehran. He nixed the five-pack of Paris Hilton scents and then we fought over Céline Dion Chic and Britney Spears Believe. Finally we settled on Elizabeth Taylor Passion in honor of the stage chicken named Liz Taylor that we hadn't chosen to hire. And because Mehran had taken to calling me Elizabeth Taylor because of all my sicknesses.

The good bath began with a shower. I had to wash myself down three times using a soap into which Mama Lola had hammered a penny. Then I gave the soap to Zaar and Vidas and again they had to drive it away and dispose of it.

Mama Lola told me to put on new underwear. Maybe it says something about my marriage that I didn't have a fresh new set of sexy or pretty lingerie. Instead I came downstairs wearing match-ing boy shorts and a racerback cashmere bra that a company had sent me.

I stood in the den on a fresh patch of newspaper. Mama Lola had a jar of healing oil and I expected her to, I don't know, maybe drip it lightly on my shoulders? Instead she went straight for my lower back. She touched my spine and said, "Does this hurt?"

I said, "Yes, it's because I'm always lifting the kids."

Mama Lola said, "Wait, lie down." I lay down on the floor, on my back. The cameras tilted down, staring at me with two big worried eyes. I looked up at Mehran. He looked down at me.

Mama Lola told me to roll over. Then, with no warning, she pulled my underwear down, exposing my ass crack to all assem-bled. If I didn't know and respect Mama Lola, I'd suspect she was being paid to create a billion-dollar scandal tape. I said, "Sorry, Ryan," to our cameraman. Ryan laughed. Apparently the embar-rassment was all mine.

Mama Lola was examining me from top to bottom. When she came to my tailbone, she said, "Oh my God!" Mehran said later he was sure she'd found an evil spirit in my ass. But Mama Lola had just discovered that my tailbone was crooked, something I've known for a while.

Just then Scout and Bill came in—Great! More people to join the party!—and everyone took turns feeling my tailbone.

Mehran said, "It's like you have a tail."

Bill said, "You're turning into a reptile. It's because you're obsessed with *V*."

Scout said it was from all the flying splits I did in the nineties. Maybe he was onto something. When I was in my ex-husband Charlie's play *Maybe Baby, It's You*, I did the flying splits four nights a week for four months straight.

Mama Lola ignored the wisecracking. She said, "Get me a leaf." She stuck the leaf to my jutting tailbone with some healing oil, then used an Ace bandage to hold the leaf firmly in place. She told me that because of this complication she would have to stay two extra days to complete her work. Then she plopped down on the couch to watch *Oprah*. Mama Lola's work for the day was done.

Okay, this may be hard to believe, but lifting the evil eye didn't seem to help my headache. Maybe we should have slaughtered the chicken. (I would never.)

A few days later our friend Scott, who races with Dean and Santiago, saw me walking around the house with my headache relief roll-on stick. He said that his ex-girlfriend was an energy healer and past life worker, or something like that, living in Hawaii. Of course! My energy needed healing! Plus, I figured my past lives must have some ideas about how to fix the headaches. Why keep hunting for a solution when Lady Victoria Spellingshire might have solved it with some vinegar and opium poultices back in the Middle Ages? I couldn't say no.

Scott called her and asked if she could do some energy healing on me. She said that she could do it over the phone, without even talking to me, if I just gave my permission. It was random and very long-distance, but I had nothing to lose except cell phone minutes. I gave Scott my permission, and an hour later she called back with the results.

Scott was on the phone with her, relaying what she said while I sat there awkwardly, feeling too shy to talk to her directly, occasionally wondering if it would be rude to tweet while he communicated my reading (answer: yes), and then wondering if I should go ahead and do it anyway (answer: again yes).

His ex-girlfriend told Scott that she saw a lot of pain radiating from the top of my head, and she knew why. She explained that Dean had been my husband in a past life—that we had been married before. I perked up. Of course that made perfect sense. No wonder we were soul mates. We both felt the powerful pull of our ancient love affair, back when we hung out in the Byzantine Empire and were followed around by a cart of scribes with large stone tablets, chiseling out our every move for the public to read about later.

But what was she saying now? I snapped out of my fantasy to

hear Scott report that Dean had cheated on me in a past life, and I had caught him and confronted him. Oh. My momentary enthusiasm for this past life reading disappeared, but she wasn't done. Apparently, in this past life Dean and I had gotten into a fight over his infidelity that ended with him hitting me on top of my head and killing me. Hence the headache. My head hurt where he'd whacked me. Aha! All of this was Dean's fault! No wonder women get more migraines than men!

I said, perhaps not entirely accurately, "That makes perfect sense." It did play into some of my fears. Given our history, I often get worried that Dean is going to cheat on me. If the phone rings and it's a girl's voice, I have to ask if he's having an affair. Dean has never been anything but devoted, and he tells me over and over again that he would never do that. Deep down I believe him. Dean would never hurt me like that. But I can't stop myself. For some reason I'm compelled to accuse him of cheating. Now I had an excuse . . . er, I mean, an *explanation*. Scott's ex-girlfriend told me that the subconscious doesn't know the difference between the present life and past lives. So I was confusing my Dean in this life with the past Dean, the Dean who was a cheater. That's why I kept accusing him. The only part that didn't quite make sense was that he defended himself so vigorously. Didn't his own subconscious feel guilty for his past crimes of passion?

Poor Dean happened to walk into this scene. I said, "Thanks a lot. You cheated on me. You killed me. And you're causing these headaches. Now I have to give myself permission to be in this lifetime and forgive you for killing me in a past life."

Dean looked from me to Scott to the phone and said, "I'm going to come back later."

But the headaches continued. Eventually Western medicine had a theory about my headaches. The pain doctor thought that they could be due to compression in my cervical (neck) vertebrae.

So I checked into the hospital as an outpatient to have a nerve block injected into my spine. Holiday cheer, holiday cheer all around! I would be numb in that area from within. Any relief would be temporary, but if the pain subsided, it would tell us that we'd found the problem.

Waiting to be sedated, I lay on a gurney in a lovely Tiffany blue hospital cap listening to Christmas carols play on the nurse's laptop. It was a small procedure, so Dean was with Stella at school. I was obsessing about my unfinished Christmas list when the doctor rushed past, pausing to announce, "You're next on the runway!" Did he say *runway*? The airplane association made me break into a nervous sweat. I distracted myself by pretending he was alluding to a fashion runway. It was Fashion Week. Heroin chic was over. We were here to launch a new fashion trend. This was the H1N1 Anorexic B List Reality Collection debut and I was the star model! Boy, did I work that IV in my head! And then they came for me . . .

They brought me into the operating room, all the while calling me "Ms. Birkin," the false name I used when I'm trying to avoid "Tori Spelling" attention. (It's a little more subtle than the "Victoria Spellman" alias I was given in jury duty.) So all the hospital employees kept calling me "Ms. Birkin" with a wink-wink in their voices, since they all knew I was Tori.

I was worried about the sedation. The anesthesiologist said that most people liked being sedated during procedures. Well, not me. I'm a Taurus! I can't delegate a single email about scheduling or edits to the show; how am I supposed to delegate my consciousness? As the nurse started my IV drip, I couldn't help myself. In rapid-fire babble I started in: "I don't think I need to be completely sedated perhaps just a light twilight will do because you know I am very small so maybe just a little and maybe you didn't realize that I can hold my neck really really still so do I really need sedation at all?" The last thing I remember hearing before I went under was my own loud, panicked voice desperately proclaiming, "I just don't like being out of control, guys!"

Next thing I knew I awoke to "Ms. Birkin?" I opened my eyes and tried to focus on the nurse's face. She said, "The procedure went well." Then she paused and her two blurred faces melded into one clear face with a knowing smile. She added, "You were very talkative."

Talkative? What exactly did that mean? What had I revealed? Did I reveal that I was nervous because I was soon to go to a Christmas party at the home of my estranged mother? Did I mention that my reality show filmed a voodoo high priestess making me wipe my wootle with a rag after she bathed me in gin, dried beans, and cheap Mexican perfume because I believed my husband's ex-wife had put a hex on me? Did the nurse mean talkative as in "You should promptly call your entertainment lawyer and request that a nondisclosure be faxed to the hospital for all witnesses to sign"?

Then bits and pieces started coming back to me. I remembered that I'd told them about my rescue dogs. That dirty secret. And there was more. I had told them I like to . . . bake! And that I was hoping to have time this crazy holiday season to make homemade marshmallows. There it was: my deepest secrets were out of the bag. Put a little truth serum in me and you'll find out that Tori Spelling goes by Chloe Birkin, rescues dogs in her spare time, and would rather not use packaged marshmallows anymore. Somebody phone the tabloids. Put me on the line. I'll tell them the dirtiest secret of all: my wootle was still raw (yet flowery-smelling) from Mama Lola's bath.

I came home from the spinal block in worse shape than ever. Later that night, after the kids were in bed, I was feeling so lost that I walked into my closet. Surrounding myself in high fashion—that had to make me feel better. I sat on the floor, looking up at flowy Zandra Rhodes caftans, Missoni tunics, Marc Jacobs jewel tone shift dresses, and my prized Chanel tweed blazers sprinkled among Forever 21 and Topshop T-shirts and tanks. I was so sick of being sick. You know it's a low moment if Christian Louboutin doesn't cheer you up. I was at my wits' end.

I sat down on the floor of the closet, crying a little, wondering what would give me the strength to get through this. Then I saw something behind the door. *Ooh, my Lanvin bag. I haven't seen that in a while. So chic!* When I change purses, I never clean them out. Coming back to them, I'm always amazed at what I find. Once I found all of Liam's ultrasound pictures in a quilted vintage Chanel bag. Now, still sniffling, I reached into the Lanvin bag, wondering what I might find—some symbol to give me the strength I needed? I pulled out my hand to find myself holding a baby toy. It was a clip-on stroller toy, a cluster of black and white plastic disks with faces on them. It had been Liam's, then Stella's, but I hadn't seen it since she was an infant. Suddenly it was in my hand, and the word *babies* floated out of my mouth. My strength was my babies. I know it sounds like a revelation-in-the-closet scene from a cheesy daytime drama, but it happened and it was pretty magical.

I was reveling in the moment when Dean happened to come into our closet. I scared the shit out of him. I told him what had happened. And then I said, "I'm being sent signs! What else do you think is in here?" I dug in the purse, certain that whatever I pulled out next would be another symbol of strength, a sign to guide me onward. It was . . . a CVS receipt for Gas-X. Okay, spirits, very funny.

I miss you, Uncle Danny.

Kate Moss, watch out!

Motorcycle Madness

Okay, he's *hot* in leather . . . but still too dangerous.

Go, Daddy, go!

Clearly I am outvoted.

My family—
blood and found.

Mehran: the Will to my Grace.

Nobody puts
Stella in a corner!

Liam enjoys one of
his "uncles" on our
TV crew.

We play hard . . .

love harder . . .

and then
decompress with
a tubby at the end
of the day!

Siblings at Play

A Candyland Christmas

Dressed to impress.

Meet the McDermotts.

My true love.

Conquering my fears—sorta.

My blessed life.

Have Yourself a
Merry Little Reconciliation

My mother and I have our challenges, and external forces weren't on our side. My first admission to the hospital was on the news, so my mother found out about it. It turned out that my mother was hospitalized at the same time, having surgery on her back. My mother's assistant reached out to me, saying that my mother wanted to know if I was okay and wondering if we were in the same hospital. We weren't, but I appreciated the gesture. I asked her assistant what kind of flowers my mother liked best these days and ordered white roses to be sent to her room with a get-well card from Liam and Stella.

Two weeks later I got an email from my mother's assistant. It said, "I remember you asked me what flowers your mother currently likes so you could send some. I just wanted to check with you because she never received anything." The flowers had never arrived. I called the florist to find out what had happened. They told me that they had tried to make the delivery, but my mother had already been released from the hospital. Then they tried to call me but had an out-of-date phone number. Shit. Maybe my mother and I just weren't destined to connect, no matter how we tried. I re-sent the flowers and asked the florist to write a note so my mother knew I had made the earlier effort.

While I was in the hospital that first time, I received an invitation to my mother's Christmas party. She had invited us for Liam's first Christmas, but we'd been in Toronto. This year I wanted to go. The kids had such a nice visit with her in the fall. I knew Liam remembered her. I wanted to build their relationship, or at least to facilitate it.

Now, mere days after my unsuccessful spinal block, the party was upon us. I had RSVP'd yes for the whole family weeks earlier, but I hadn't told any of my friends we planned to see my mother. This was admittedly odd behavior on my part, since I usually overshare my mom stuff with my friends. (Or maybe what's odd is the oversharing, but either way my tight-lipped approach was out of character.) The only friend I told was Mehran. Mehran has always been a huge advocate for my mother. He has a great relationship with his own mother, and he always encourages me to reach out to mine. Deep down I think I told Mehran and Mehran alone because I knew he'd approve. My other friends might be more cautious because of the roller-coaster relationship I have with my mother.

On the morning of the party Scout emailed to ask what we were doing that night. I wrote, "Did I bury the lead and not tell you? We're going to my mom's Christmas party. I don't know why I didn't tell you guys. Clearly I still have issues."

To my surprise, Scout wrote back, "I think it's a good thing and the right thing." Even Dean, who was always cautious and protective of me when it came to my mother, was completely supportive.

My mother's knowledge of proper party etiquette would give Emily Post a run for her money. I learned everything I know about planning parties from Candy Spelling and I'm no slouch. So of course the day of the party I knew to prepare a hostess gift. I'd never show up without one. I planned to give her something safe—pictures of the kids from the Little Maven photo shoot in simple silver frames. Easy enough, but there was no way I was going to gift-wrap the photos myself. My mother's gift-wrapping room in the Manor wasn't just for show. She is a world-class gift wrapper.

It was pouring the day of the party, but I dragged the entire family to a nice paper store nearby called Papyrus. I went directly to the counter and asked to see their fanciest paper. There were beautiful single sheets that they kept behind the counter, but they weren't broad enough to wrap the 8 × 10 picture without using more than one sheet. Multiple sheets meant there would be seams. Seams were unacceptable. The woman behind the counter helped me find some paper that would work. It was from a package roll (imagine!), but it was embossed with raised gold elements. Candy would like that.

Then I needed really nice ribbon to make big bows. The clerk showed me a pretty ribbon, but it didn't have wire to give the bows shape. I said, "Don't I need a ribbon with wire? For a big, structured bow?" I looked like a nervous freak, but a floppy bow would not do. My mother wasn't going to go Joan Crawford over the wire ribbon, but I knew she'd appreciate a well-wrapped gift.

Getting the gifts wrapped consumed a huge part of the day. Liam, Stella, and Jack were with us, and Dean juggled the little ones in the store while I worked on the wrapping. Dean was so sweet, as patient as can be. He got that it was important.

We put the kids down for their naps on the late side because the party didn't start until seven-thirty, which was Stella's bedtime. With late naps we would aim to stay at the party for a good hour. Stella had never seen the hour of nine p.m. in all her short life.

While the kids napped I decided to curl my hair. The whole process took two hours as I sectioned off parts and curled them one by one. As I labored, I was checking emails and tweets. Scout texted me, "What are you wearing and how are you wearing your hair?"

I wrote back, "I'm curling it as we speak, but what about the rain?" And how would my mother react? Would she think I was too old for long, loose curls? Would wearing it up be more lady-like? But that seemed too conservative for me. Scout suggested a side bun. He said it was chic. So I pulled it over to the side and put most of it up with a thick curl hanging down.

Then I had to decide what dress to wear. I wanted Stella to look perfect for the party. I had ordered her dress from the Nordstrom website a month before the party—the top was black velvet and the bottom was tartan taffeta—but I hadn't given any thought to what I myself would wear. I couldn't bring myself to shop for the night. If I did, it would feel like I was trying too hard, building my own expectations, getting my hopes up.

Instead, now that the night was upon me, I started trying on dresses that I already owned. I started with red—it was Christmas, after all—but then I got nervous about wearing red because I didn't want my mother or anyone else to think I was trying to steal the show. I decided to play it safe and wear a black dress with subdued red lipstick. I must have tried on a total of eight dresses. At least. All of a sudden I felt like I was sixteen again, getting ready to go out with the family, wanting to please my mother.

When Liam woke up I dressed him in a tartan shirt, a vest, and a blazer. Jack wore a tie and blazer. Stella is obsessed with purses, thanks to Uncle Danny, who sent her her first purse, so in my closet I found a small Chanel satin purse—a mini bag with a handle—that my mother had given me years before. It had the little Chanel camellia and black rhinestones. For Stella it was a full-sized over-the-shoulder purse. She took it and put it over her shoulder, where she would keep it in perfect position the entire evening. Dean was wearing a black Jil Sander suit and a festive Dolce & Gabbana striped shirt. With everyone in their Christmas best, we all gathered at the front door to go. It had to be the best we've ever collectively looked.

On the way to the party it was still pouring, Los Angeles's biggest rain of the year, a year that was coming to a close. As Dean drove us to Holmby Hills, I started thinking about the last time I'd been at my parents' house, "the Manor." It was three and a half years earlier, for my father's funeral. When I had wanted to leave, my friends and I had made our exit by climbing over the backyard hedges just in order to avoid going back through the house and saying good-bye to my mother. When I left the Manor that time, I thought I would never return.

All the power was out in Holmby Hills because of the rain. Even the streetlights were out. The streets were slick with rain, shiny and deserted. Dean said, "The lights are out. Do you think she has a generator?"

I didn't pause to consider. I said, "Of course she has a generator."

We drove through the darkness. Then, as we neared the house, we saw it through the pouring rain. There it was, the Manor, lit by a city's worth of Christmas lights. Had my mother planned the whole power outage to highlight the Manor in all its Christmas glory? We drove up the circular driveway. It was illuminated by projections of snowflakes that moved across the pavement— huge snowflakes of light that must have been shining down from spotlights hidden somewhere on the roof of the house. It was magical.

Lined up on my mother's wide front steps were fifty or more oversized nutcrackers of varying heights, like a chorus of children. We walked through an aisle between the rows of nutcrackers and into the front hall. There we were met by the sound of Christmas carolers. Not only that, but people dressed as toy soldiers marching in formation up, down, and around the sweeping double staircase that framed the foyer. It was brilliant, a stunning welcome that was Christmassy and original, but repetitive enough that people wouldn't linger to watch it for so long that they caused a traffic jam. The kids loved it. From a party planning perspective I was in awe.

I turned to Dean and whispered, "This isn't like the Christmas parties we had growing up." Holiday parties were always a tradition in our house. We had one every year until my dad got sick, but Dean had never been to one. My friends still talk about the legend of the Spelling Christmas Eve party, but the truth is that they weren't huge parties—maybe thirty or forty close friends and business executives. In later years, when Randy was still at home and I had already moved out, Nanny, who was by then in her seventies, would show up wearing a festive Christmas sweater and ornament earrings and carrying her own Bloody Mary mix. She'd hand the bottle to the bartender and proceed to get wasted. One year Randy and I made Nanny smoke pot. For the most part those parties were fun and extravagant, but not *produced*.

This year Randy had written to prepare me that the party would be different, implying that it wasn't just a small family party, and as I peered in I saw that he wasn't kidding. The place was already crowded. There must have been two hundred people there. My friends and I always wondered why my parents never threw huge parties with a house like that. It must have been because my dad never wanted parties. This was my mother's forte. I looked at my children gazing in wonder at the live toy soldiers. Wouldn't it have been cool to grow up with parties like this? Then again, when I was growing up I always yearned for small and homegrown. It probably would have been too much for me.

In the foyer I was greeted by a familiar face. It was Mindy, the party planner who had worked on my wedding to Charlie. She gave me a hug and asked, "Are you okay?"

I said, "Yeah, I am. I'm glad you're here." She knew better than anyone here what the dynamic had been between me and my mother. She'd seen firsthand the fights we had while we planned my wedding. She had some idea of what this night was about.

Mindy took our coats and Stella's diaper bag. I could do without it: we wouldn't be here long enough to need a change. I carried Stella; Dean was with Liam and Jack. The hallway was packed. Then my mother appeared out of nowhere. As she walked over to us, the first thing I noticed—the first thing any of us noticed—was that she and Stella were in matching dresses. My mother's had white on top and Stella's had black. But their skirts were identical tartan taffeta.

I had been nervous for weeks about this moment. I hadn't seen my mother in two years. In that time we had done nothing to fix our relationship. I'm the queen of nonconfrontation. This was a major moment. And yet, as she approached us and I found myself just seconds away from seeing her again, I wasn't crazy scared. She was my mother. Something told me it was going to be fine.

The first thing Mom said was "Look! Stella! We have the same dress on."

Thank God for that dress. It was a perfect icebreaker for me and my mother, and it set the right tone. We were family. We were all in the Christmas spirit. We would always have something in common whether we planned it or not.

From then on, the whole night, people would see the two dresses and ask me, "Did you guys plan that?" Everyone thought my mother and I had had a huge reunion. They were probably picturing the two of us going to lunch and shopping for dresses together when the reality was that we'd only emailed a handful of times in the past year. But I wasn't about to announce that Stella's dress was $39.99 at Nordstrom online. Stella's purse, which she continued to carry with pride, also drew a lot of attention. Every lady there said, "It's a Chanel purse!" I quickly said, "It's mine. I loaned it to her." I didn't want them to think I'd bought an eighteen-month-old a Chanel purse.

After my mother marveled over her granddaughter twin and the boys, she came in to hug me. She smiled at me. There was no moment of discomfort. No awkward pause where I had to think about what to do or say. It was very warm and natural. Well, except that as soon as we hugged, it seemed like the whole party stopped talking and looked over. Even the bartenders froze, bottles mid-pour (or so it seemed to me). All eyes were on us. But at least I was used to that. I thought, *Wow. This private moment is finally happening in public.* But it didn't feel weird. It felt like it was exactly as it should be. I couldn't imagine anything being different.

That's not to say that everything was magically fine and dandy, as if there had never been a rift between me and my mother. I have many fears, but I've never been afraid of giving my heart to other people. My whole life I've prided myself on believing in love. No matter how many times I got hurt, I never gave up on love. Boyfriend after boyfriend, I always came back to love with open arms and eyes wide open. I loved again like I'd never been hurt. Now, when my mother hugged me, it was as if I was watching myself in a movie, and I could tell that I had a wall up. I can't speak for her, but I felt that she was more engaged, more willing to give than I was. My smile and eyes were there, nobody else would have seen or felt the difference, but I knew there was a wall of protection. I was responding to everything she said, but I could hear that my voice wasn't as warm as it usually is. It felt different, like for the first time—maybe in my life—I was cautious about love.

My mother was in the middle of hosting a fancy, fabulous party. She had caterers, entertainers, and tons of guests to attend to. But she was extremely attentive to and doting on us. There were people there from networks, gossip columns, and the enter-tainment industry—in front of them and all her friends she was going to be gracious no matter what—but her behavior toward us felt completely real to me.

I assumed that encountering my mother would be the hardest part of the party for me, but it wasn't. It was her friends. I feel fond toward my mother's friends, and we hadn't seen each other in years, but tonight each and every friend wanted the chance to talk to me, to say, "I'm so happy you're here. This is the right thing." I know they spoke out of affection for my mother, but she and I hadn't really talked or worked anything out. Maybe we wouldn't. Maybe we would just move past our troubles without hashing them out. But even if that was the case, our reconciliation was in progress. It was happening at that very moment! I was still in the middle of seeing my mother for the first time, and everyone was already patting me on the back about it.

I got stuck in the foyer. It happens to me at every party, and just because this was my mother's house, a house where I'd lived, the house where I'd gotten married for the first time, a place I'd been umpteen times, that night was no exception. It was kind of like being in a formal receiving line. As soon as I finished talking to one person, another approached me. I had no time to take a step toward, say, that Christmassy cocktail I imagined would take the edge off the tension of this night. It felt like I was working, as if I'd been hired to come to a party and greet every single person there. While carrying my baby girl for the first time since I'd had a spinal block. And wearing four-inch Louboutin heels. I don't usually wear heels and carry Stella. She's heavy. It never occurred to me that it would be so crowded and we would be so stuck. It took me the first forty-five minutes of the party to inch from the foyer into the formal living room. Back when I lived here, I would have kicked off those increasingly painful heels, but tonight I was a guest in this house.

Meanwhile, where was Dean? I had no idea. He had disappeared into the party with Liam and Jack. He ditched me and Stella! I kept glancing over shoulders trying to catch sight of him, hoping to hand over Stella, score a drink, or just make contact with a familiar face, but no such luck. Then I did see a friendly face, but it wasn't Dean. It was Mindy, the party planner. She asked if there was anything she could get me. I said, "Where's Dean? Where's my husband?" Mindy volunteered to hunt him down and disappeared into the throngs.

I kept eyeing the formal living room, which was my short-term goal: it wasn't so crowded, and there was a good chance a waiter would come around passing food or drinks. In between each well-wishing friend of Mom's, I managed to take a step or two toward it. There would be relief, solace, a chair. I got closer, closer; just one or two more "I am so happy to see you here," and I'd be in. But suddenly someone materialized right in front of me. He announced, "I'm the fastest Etch A Sketcher in the world," and asked to do a portrait of me and Stella on a travel-sized Etch A Sketch. So I posed for his portrait as people continued to chat with me. Now I was wearing heels, holding Stella, chatting, and all the while trying to keep my face turned to the perfect angle so the Etch A Sketcher captured my good side. Fifteen minutes later—speedy for the artist but a lifetime for that contorted pose!—I had a pretty impressive portrait. I'm just grateful my mom didn't hire the slowest Etch A Sketcher in the world.

I finally made it into the formal living room, although just before going down the steps to the sunken living room, Stella found a little scene made of wood with Santa riding a Christmas sleigh, fake snow, and a chest with tiny toys peeking out. Stella pulled the rocking horse off. Oops. I said, "We need to put that back, Mamita. That's Grandma's."

The formal living room was as large as a hotel lobby, decorated in creams and satins with couches and low tables. Just as we entered, Mindy came back. She said, "Dean and the boys are downstairs bowling." Of course. Only in the Manor.

I said, "Do you know how scary this night is for me and he's abandoned me?" The truth was that I was doing fine emotionally, but Dean didn't know that. Shouldn't he be checking in on me?

Stella was not interested in the formal living room. Instead, she pulled me toward the kitchen. There some of the uniformed staff were plating food and cleaning dishes. Stella laid on the charm with the staff, showing off her purse and demo-ing the little plastic Mickey Mouse cell phone she had tucked inside. I looked down at her and saw that this was where she was most content. Not at the fancy party but among the warm, friendly staff. I understood completely. That was me as a kid.

On our way back to the party Stella detoured into the powder room, which was a mother's nightmare. It was full of tiny, breakable tchotchkes, Limoges boxes, silk chairs, all at Stella's level. I said, "Don't touch anything!" and whisked her out of there as fast as I could. Every mother has had this party experience, led by your small child into random nooks of someone else's house, hoping nothing gets broken, scoping out the two-foot-high world alongside your child as a lovely party—food, drinks, music, conversation—beckons just out of reach.

I thought of a compromise and steered Stella toward the other living room, the informal family room where we used to have our Christmas parties when I was a kid and where the Christmas tree always stood. There was a fireplace, a piano, and there, in a wood-paneled alcove that looked like it was designed exclusively for this purpose (and maybe it was), sat the eighteen-foot Christmas tree. I saw an empty chair in the corner, near the fireplace. My poor feet silently chanted, "Go! Go! Go!" and I made a beeline for the chair, but someone sat in it just before I got there. Mindy, the wedding planner, appeared like an angel with a plate of food for Stella. All the other chairs seemed to be occupied, so the three of us sat on the floor in the corner near the fireplace while I fed Stella. I wouldn't want to feed her near my mom's silk upholstery anyway.

Then I turned and saw my brother, Randy, approaching. We hugged, I introduced him to Stella, and I met his girlfriend Leah. I hadn't seen Randy since Liam was an infant. He looked different, older. Two years is a long time. Just as I'd been busy raising my kids, his life had gone on without me in it. Seeing my brother was in some ways more intense than seeing my mom. I knew he was more likely to want to talk things through. But at the same time it made the place feel like home. He was my brother. I was so happy he was there. At events like this my brother had always been my connection to normalcy. Now he was holding Stella with a big smile on his face. I could tell he was into seeing her. She was looking back at him, giggling as if she recognized him as family. I looked at Randy's hands: they were hands I'd known for most of my life, I knew them so well, but I didn't recognize them anymore. Did his hands change in two years, or had I forgotten them? We'd been so close. We were best friends. Then life went a certain way. It made me sad.

The Christmas tree was enormous and beautifully, amazingly, immaculately decorated. When Stella finally noticed it (it takes the kids a while to process everything in the room), she stood frozen, just staring at it. I watched her. Then, as I watched, she started grabbing ball ornaments and pulling them. I dove in, but before I reached her she managed to pull one off the loop from which it hung.

I said, "Shoot, you busted Grandma's ball." No joke intended. I was treading carefully tonight. I didn't want anything to go wrong. So far everything had been perfect (except for Stella trying to pilfer that little rocking horse). Now Stella had broken a ball, upsetting the perfect design of the tree. I looked up to see if anyone had noticed. There, at a two-top table right in front of me was none other than Sean Hayes. Oh my God, Sean Hayes! I loved *Will & Grace*. I'm a huge fan of his. Sean Hayes had seen Stella break the ball. What would he think? What did I know about Sean Hayes? Was he discreet or would Sean Hayes rat me out to my mother? Should I say anything? At a loss, I took the ball and shoved it into the depths of the Christmas tree. There, that didn't look so bad. I started to turn back to Sean Hayes to make an excuse, but as I started to speak, Stella grabbed another ball and broke it too. She obviously had a grand plan here. Maybe she was taking preemptive revenge on me for grounding her from some future party as punishment for missing her curfew. I'm sorry, future Stella, but actions have consequences. Period.

Suddenly my mother swooped in, saying, "We should take a family photo." I was holding the second broken ball, the evidence of my offspring's crime and our future friction.

I said, "I'm so sorry. Stella broke your ball."

My mother held out her hand. "Here, give it to me." Really? She was going to take the broken ball?

I said, "I'll throw it away."

She said, "Don't be silly. Give it to me." My mom's ex, Mark, had once quoted her as saying, "I hope if I have grandchildren, they don't break anything in my house." But now I wondered if she'd ever really said it because that wasn't her attitude at all. She was acting like the broken ball was no big deal. Here she was, elegantly dressed, hosting a party, and holding out her hand for the ornament. It was so momlike. And for me, that was it. That was the moment when I was drawn in. The wall came down and I smiled. This was what I wanted most of all, for myself and for my kids. A mother. A grandmother.

Dean finally came back. Smart man, he showed up when enough people were around that I couldn't give him what for. I just whispered, "You left me for so long."

He said, "Jack and Liam were loving the bowling alley."

I repeated, "You left me for so long." And then I added, "But I'm fine." It was as if Dean knew to leave me alone with Mom long enough for this to happen. He gave me a look that said, "Of course you're fine."

We took some family photos in front of the tree. My mother held Stella. I worried about her back—she'd just had surgery—and Stella didn't tolerate the photographer for long. Stella lunged backward and I cringed. My mom's poor back. But she didn't seem to mind.

After we took photos of the family in various combinations, Mom said, "I want the kids to meet Santa." She went to fetch the Santa actor while I prepped Liam so he wasn't scared when he appeared. No need to worry. Liam went right up to Santa and said, "Hi. I want a monster." Then he roared a terrible roar. I went to get Stella from Dean, and as we came back I saw Liam, still engaging Santa in some in-depth conversation, most likely about the subtleties of monster toys.

I only realized how hungry I was when my brother nudged me and said that there was a seafood bar in the projection room. I knew what that meant. When we were growing up, the seafood bar was a staple at my parents' parties. There would be a silver container with ice, and platters of crab claws, shrimp, and caviar. But just as I made my way there, a man came up to me and introduced himself as the voice coach for a Broadway play called *Promises, Promises* that my mother was producing with Kristin Chenoweth and Sean Hayes. As we were talking, Sean Hayes came up to say hello.

I was completely starstruck by Sean Hayes. In my head I was saying, "Be funny. Be funny," but all I came out with was "Hi. This is Stella." Wow. Scintillating. We talked for a moment, then Sean Hayes turned away from me. I'd lost him. Mehran was going to plotz when he heard I'd met Sean Hayes. He was a gay hero. I basically consider myself a gay man inside. I wanted to be loud and proud with him—that's what I do best with my gays—except I couldn't be gay with Sean Hayes because he wasn't out. Whichever. So I didn't want to mention anything gay, but that's all I knew to talk to him about, so I couldn't talk to him at all. At the same time I couldn't walk away letting Sean Hayes think I had nothing to say. So I poked his shoulder and said, "Excuse me, I just want to tell you that I'm a huge fan and I had nothing to say to you because I couldn't speak." At least I would have some kind of interaction to report back to Mehran. I actually desperately wanted to whip out my BlackBerry and take a picture of him with me and Stella to send to Scout and Bill, but I was scared security (probably some of the same guys who'd protected my safety once upon a time) would throw me out.

Sean Hayes was perfectly gracious. He said, "Thanks for having me."

Still trying in vain to be minorly humorous, I said, "Well, it's

not like it's my house, although it's so big I could move back
in and they'd never notice." I wanted him to be Jack, whom I'd
watched on *Will & Grace* for so many years that I felt he was one
of mine. We'd link arms and trot around the Christmas tree and
it would be fabulous. But he didn't say, "I loved you in the movie
Trick," which meant he probably wasn't even closeted gay. I have
yet to meet a gay man who didn't love that movie, and me in it.
That role is my virtual gaydar. Some time after the party Sean
Hayes came out. I guess that makes him—and *Variety*—the only
ones who didn't appreciate that performance.

I made some crack about Stella crapping her pants (which did
get a laugh out of the voice coach) and went to find Dean so
he could take both kids while I found myself something to eat.
But Sean Hayes was the highlight of my night. Dramatic family
reunions and reconciliations aside.

The seafood buffet was set up in the projection room, which
looks like a massive living room unless the full-sized movie screen
that rises up from the floor at one end has been elevated. At the
opposite end of the room the art rises like in some spy movie to
reveal holes in the wall through which the projectionist screens
the movie from his own little projection room. In between are
comfortable chairs and tables, all of which can rotate to face the
screen. Tonight the art and all the furnishings were in living room
formation, with the seafood buffet at one end. Oh, I was so close
to the buffet. I could see it. I could almost taste it. I hadn't had
a bite to eat all night. This was my chance. I was steps away. But
just then a seated woman stuck out her hand and grabbed my

arm. I stopped in my tracks. She said, "Hi. I play mah-jongg with your mother." She was perched comfortably on a chair, a heaping plate of food on her lap. She had shrimp cocktail and huge crab legs. I think I started salivating. The woman went on to say, "You and I used to go to Rosanna together at Fantastic Sam's." I remembered Rosanna. She worked at the Fantastic Sam's in Beverly Hills and did the best blow-out in town for twenty-five dollars until *Allure* featured her in "Best Beauty Tips." Then people caught on and she left to open her own salon. The mah-jongg woman said, "Where do you get blow-outs now?"

I said, "I don't get blow-outs anymore."

She looked at me, perplexed, and took another bite of her delicious-looking food. Was that a little pile of caviar? "Well, someone does your hair. I mean, you had your hair done tonight."

I said, "I did my own hair."

She said, "Oh, okay." She clearly didn't believe me. Then, as if she'd figured it all out, she said, "Do you need someone?" If I didn't have someone to do my hair, it must mean that I needed someone to do my hair.

I said, "Actually, I don't even get my nails done anymore. It's really good to see you, but I haven't had food all night."

Between bites she said, "Oh, you should. It's really good."

I was kind of proud that she didn't believe I'd done my own hair. I must have done a good job. Scout would be proud. I went straight to the seafood buffet and picked up a plate. In it I saw my shiny reflection. It was my night. The hair and makeup gods were on my side. I had wanted everything to be perfect for my mom.

I know she didn't need me to be perfect. And sure, it was kind of sad that I wanted that kind of attention from her. But at least I felt really good about myself.

I love caviar. I stood there looking at it. There were three big tins of Beluga caviar. I knew that each tin cost roughly a thousand dollars. As I stood there, the caterer replaced an empty one. I had some idea of how many tins of caviar my mother's guests would go through at a party this big. Oh my gosh, it would cost thousands of dollars in caviar alone. Last New Year's Eve I had gone to the local cheese shop and splurged on an ounce of caviar for me and Dean. It cost one hundred fifty dollars, but it was a special occasion. Here, the caterers were replacing the large empty tin as if it were nothing.

The woman serving the caviar bar was wearing a white jacket and bow tie. She was young and pleasant. I didn't see the toast points my parents always had at their seafood bars. I looked for their suitable replacement. I said, "Excuse me, I'm looking for the, for the . . ." Duh, I couldn't think of the word.

She said, "Blinis?" Suddenly I had the same out-of-place feeling I used to have when I went shopping in my *90210* days, that Julia Roberts in *Pretty Woman* moment of looking like I was some silly girl who couldn't afford to be shopping at Gucci. I felt like I didn't belong. I don't know why.

I panicked, blabbering, "Yes, sorry, I have mommy brain. I thought those were corn cakes."

She gave me a look as if to say, "I don't care. I just work here."

But I kept going. "Um, do you happen to have the crème

fraîche? *See? You thought I was going to say sour cream. I do know the right terminology for a caviar spread.*

She said, "No, but we have an avocado mousse." Growing up we had the caviar, toast points, chopped egg, chopped onion, and lemon wedges. I was expecting that because that's how we did it. Now everything was different and I was thrown.

Submitting to the new seafood buffet, I brought my pile of caviar, my fluffy blinis, and a scoop of wasabi caviar over to where my brother was sitting on a windowsill with his girlfriend. This huge room, with all its sumptuous sofas, and they were huddled in the corner with the houseplants, away from everyone. Leah smiled and said, "Nobody puts Baby in a corner." As far as I was concerned, it was the best seat in the house. I scooted in right next to Leah.

The three of us sat there. I looked down at the caviar and said, "This isn't how I remember it."

My brother said, "But the crab claws are the same." Then he said, "Do you still like to cook? Leah's a great baker."

I said, "Mom always said, 'You're either a baker or a cooker.' I mean a cook. That was stupid, but you know what I mean."

Randy said, "What do you cook?"

I said, "Lots of stuff Nanny made us growing up. Ground beef with frozen petite peas. Shepherd's pie. Except I can't make shepherd's pie anymore because it's minorly cursed such that when I make it, I end up in the hospital."

Randy chuckled and said, "Do you make Nanny's chicken dumplings?"

I said, "No, but I make her chili and the beef stew." Randy and I were bonding again over what we knew, and Randy was just smiling. It was the simplest, most mundane conversation, but to us it meant the world.

On my way to find Dean and the kids, I ran into my mother. Throughout the evening she'd been solicitous, popping into my conversations to see if I was okay. She said, "Do you need help? There's a lot of staff here. They can take the kids." I said, "No thanks, Liam and Stella don't know them." Later she offered me juice for the kids. And now she came up to me and said, "I found the little wooden Santa cookie tray that you grew up with. I want to give it to the kids."

I said, "I'd love for them to have that. Thank you!" First she'd given the kids the frog I gave my father. Now she'd set aside the tray for them. She was connecting my kids to the nice traditions from my childhood.

I'd just finished my seafood plate when I remembered the dining room. The whole table, which sat at least twenty, was laden with food. There it was, the lavish buffet that had eluded me all night. But just then Mom said, "It's time. We're opening up the candy room." As I looked longingly back at the buffet, Mom led me, Dean, and the kids in the opposite direction, toward the breakfast room.

It was a small room (relatively speaking, of course), where we ate most of our meals when I lived at the Manor. In the middle was the breakfast table, which was white with fake snow. On the snow were mountains of cookies and candy, through which a real electric train circled around a track. There were desserts everywhere. Jars of candy. A doughnut maker. There was an ice cream sandwich station where they spread ice cream on any flavor of cookie and wrapped it in edible paper. Signs in the room said, "Welcome to Candyland."

My mother pointed us to certain desserts, saying, "Try this one, it has this in it, and this other one has this." She knew each dessert, and I realized that she'd had a tasting. Of course she had. She had tasted all the desserts and all the food. That was my mom.

The kids were wearing out, but Candyland gave them a second wind. I left Dean and my mom in there with them and made a break for it. I had to hit the buffet of food.

It was getting late. All the other guests had already feasted for hours, and in the dining room most of the food was gone. As I approached the table I took off my heels and slung them over my finger. I took a plate and started to serve myself. A waiter offered to help. He held the plate for me as I scooped food on, babbling apologies. "I feel really bad," I said, as I helped myself to ravioli. "This is really nice of you. I don't usually let people do things for me. I'm a mom." On I went, determined to prove that I didn't live an over-the-top life.

As I came out of the dining room with my abundant plate and my shoes still dangling from my finger, I ran into my stepson Jack holding his Candyland dessert plate. Jack had been a pleasure all night—sweet with the kids, polite, amazing. He said, "Hey, TT."

No time for small talk. I said, "I just want to eat." I led him into my father's office. There was a bar set up in there. Some guests were having drinks. My brother and Leah were on the couch getting a psychic reading. Jack and I found a good corner and sat down on the floor (again) to eat. I was starting to feel pretty comfortable there. Jack said, "Your mom's really nice."

I said, "Thanks, yeah, she is."

Jack said, "I really like her." My mother had embraced him that night. There was an opportunity for peace, for all of us.

I said, "My mother has really taken to you. She wants you to come back and bowl."

Jack said, "I like it here. Are we going to come back?"

I said, "Sure." It was a nice moment. Then the photographer started snapping pictures. I flashed back to being twenty-two, hanging out in this office with my friends, shoes off, champagne in hand, wasted. My mother was going to look through these photos, see me sitting shoeless on the floor, and think that I was drunk and had to sit down. The reality was that I hadn't had a single drink. But I'd held a twenty-one-pound child for over three hours in four-inch heels. The effects were comparable.

Holy crap, it was almost eleven o'clock. Time had flown. I couldn't believe the kids were still conscious. Dean came in and said, "We gotta go. Liam and Stella hit a wall." He hurried out to collect the kids. I said some good-byes and went out to the front. By the time I got to the now-empty foyer, Dean was on his hands and knees, wiping the carpet with baby wipes. Stella had gotten chocolate on the carpet. As he scrubbed hopelessly, Stella and Liam played with some Christmas decorations at the bottom of the staircase. My mom saw Dean cleaning and said, "Don't worry about it." This was the third time my child had attempted to destroy the Manor, but Mom was easy breezy. She'd been acting like a grandma about it from the start, and I was finally catching on. Maybe this house was child-friendly after all.

Then someone came with our coats and the diaper bag and we geared up the kids for the still-rainy night. My mother came out with two stuffed dogs that sang "Merry Christmas to You." She handed one to each child.

I was holding Stella. My mother said to her, "Can I give you a kiss good-bye?" She gave Stella an Eskimo kiss, rubbing noses with her, and a butterfly kiss, fluttering her eyelashes against Stella's. Stella giggled and giggled. I said, "I remember you used to do that with me."

My mother said, "I want to ask if you want to have Christmas dinner with Randy, Leah, and me. It will just be family. I don't even have a cook."

I said, "Dean and I weren't going to do anything. We don't have any plans."

Mom said, "Well, I was thinking of going to the Polo Lounge for dinner. Would that be okay?"

I said, "Yeah, that would be really fun."

Dean overheard and said, "Yeah, wouldn't that be nice?" Oh my God. Okay. I was going to have dinner with my family. After all these years my family would be together again for the holidays.

My mother walked us out. She gave me a hug and said, "I love you. I really love you. I hope you know that. Tonight was really special for me." She made sure I knew she meant it.

I still felt some guardedness, but I took it in. I was scared, but deep down it meant everything to me. I said, "I love you too."

As we left, we were given eye masks with cards that said "Sweet dreams" and were signed "Candy." I knew she'd carefully chosen what color pen to use for her signature. I knew she'd picked the color of the border line on the gift card. She's detail-obsessed just like me. Then, for the final touch, a guy dressed in knickers and a hat, like an old-fashioned newsboy, held out a newspaper. He said, "*New York Times*? Tomorrow's edition?"

Wow. She was a pro.

The Start of Something

O n the way home from my mother's Christmas party I was wired, but not from sugar. I was happy inside. As Dean and I went over the little details of the party, I said, "Do you hear the way I'm blabbering? I'm excited."

In the past Dean had been dismissive of my mother. He said, "If she's not worthy, cut her out. When do you stop getting hurt?" But from the moment we got the invitation to the Christmas party, he was with me. He went into it open-minded and supportive (except for when he pulled his bowling alley disappearing act). I was impressed.

Now, in the car, I said, "I did it. This was hard, but it was okay."

Dean said, "I'm really proud of you. Who knows? Maybe this is the start of something."

Dean lost his father, first to alcohol, then to death. When he divorced Mary Jo, he lost his father-in-law, "Mr. E," too. Dean and Mr. E had a nice relationship. They played golf together. I knew Dean missed that. Now he made a confession. He said, "I know this is premature, but if this all works out and we have a relationship with your mother, is it wrong that down the road I see having a relationship with her boyfriend like the one Mr. E and I had? Maybe he and I could play golf together. Maybe he and your mother would come and watch me ride my motorcycle." Roger, my mom's boyfriend, was really nice. He'd been great with the kids. True, Dean was jumping the gun. I didn't know what kind of mom my mother was going to be, much less how her boyfriend would be as a father, but Dean's fantasy swept me up immediately. Suddenly I was entertaining a double date fantasy—the four of us having dinner together. But what was wrong with that? Who's to say my mother didn't sit at home wanting the same thing? Maybe someday soon she would ride the teacups in Disneyland with Liam and Stella the way she used to with me and Randy.

There were moments, memories, traditions from my childhood that I remembered fondly. I went through a phase of having only bad recollections, but as the kids got older, going to school, having birthdays, celebrating holidays, living life with us, I started remembering the good times I had with my family. The traditions I shared with my mother came back to me. I started bringing them to the world I created for my children. My mother's hand was in the crafts, the baking, the parties that I loved doing with and for my children.

Was the person I remembered with love still there? I knew I'd seen her when my mother collected the broken Christmas balls. She was a mommy again.

Then I had a revelation. I said to Dean, "Maybe I bought into the press too much. Maybe after all is said and done, my mother and I both listened to the press and stopped having a relationship because of it." I knew we had problems. We didn't have a great relationship. But the magazines, the talk shows, the headlines about feuds, all that media attention amplified our regular problems to a crazy, impossible level.

After all these years I didn't think the press could have an effect on me. I knew the lies that were said; I knew how everything got blown out of proportion. I knew that as well or better than anyone else. *Feud* was their word, not ours. *Estranged* was their word, not ours. The press said we hated each other. We couldn't see each other. We were at war.

Our differences were real. They created a painful family dynamic. She did things I can't forget, and I'm sure she feels the same way. But a third party, the press, had made those differences harder to resolve. They elevated our struggles to a cold war, to something that felt irreconcilable. They pitted us against each other, then threw us together, over and over again. I told Dean, "I thought I was above it and beyond it and I wasn't. We could have worked on our problems, but the press distorted them. We let the press distort them. We helped it happen." We were both guilty of playing into the media's hands. Seeing the way she was that night made me feel like I'd lost two years because of the weeklies. Maybe she felt that way too.

I said, "What happens now? Is everything fine? Am I back with my mother and brother? Do I have a complete family again? Do we just move on? For the kids' sake I want to move forward. How do we do it?" I was scared. What if I got hurt again?

Dean said, "So what if you get hurt again? Better to have loved and lost than never to have loved. Better to love and get hurt than to have anger and no love." Dean was right. I had felt closed to my mother, but I was open. I had been the whole time. I smiled at Dean. I loved him so much in that moment.

I said, "Yeah, it's worth it."

During that car ride Dean and I had an amazing talk. A weight lifted off my shoulders. Dean was so understanding and patient. I felt so connected to him. He got it, everything I was feeling. He summed it up for me. He was with me going into this. We were together, side by side.

Electricity had been restored to Holmby Hills. The rain beat down on the car and shone on the streets as Dean and I drove home over the hill to our different life. All three kids were sleeping in the back seat. I knew it was the resolution of more than what we were talking about. It wasn't just about me, my mother, and my brother. It was about me and Dean.

And just like that, our ebb was flow again. We cooked together, we spent every second together. We weren't perfect. None of us were. But we were happy. I was a workaholic who tried to control far too much of my life. My headache wasn't gone. Dean still rode motorcycles. I still micromanaged the color grid of the cushions on the couch. We had more untraveled roads ahead. I would probably obsess. Dean would probably withdraw. We would fight. But we welcomed the pain; we would work through it, because it was only a part of a whole that we chose and loved almost every day.

The Metamorphosis Begins

Christmas at my mother's was a new beginning, but the rest of my life was still way out of balance. I'd tried everything—Eastern medicine, Western medicine, voodoo, phone calls to past life specialists in Hawaii, but I'd gotten no answers. I felt like giving up.

The next time I went to the pain doctor who had been treating my headaches, I said, "Why is this happening to me?"

He said, "You've lost Tori. You can't function this way. Your body is telling you to make a change."

I said, "Are you saying that I'm making myself sick? Is none of this real?"

He said, "Of course it's real. But you've been getting headaches for ten years. You've been treating the headaches. I want to know what happened ten years ago when they started."

Not to be melodramatic, but I gasped. I knew exactly what had happened ten years earlier: *90210* had ended. Being on the show was the only life I had known for ten years, starting at age sixteen. I went in a girl and was expected to come out a woman. In some ways I did. But it was also kind of like being pushed out of the nest and expected to fly with no safety net. My headaches had emerged then and never gone away.

The doctor told me that I had to reevaluate my life. I needed to find myself again.

That resonated with me. I was beginning to get why I was sick and how much would have to change if I was ever going to get better. If I looked deep enough into the psychological side of my illness, I knew exactly what I'd find. It wasn't rocket science. I was exhausted. I was working too hard and I had no one but myself to blame.

But, especially given how crappy I felt, I didn't know how to start fixing myself. Was I supposed to put "change life" on my calendar? How much time should I block out for it? A two-hour window before lunch?

I texted Mehran, who has all the answers most of the time. Or most of the answers all the time. I wrote, "There has to be an answer here. Energy work?" In a flash, Mehran, ever resourceful, texted back with a recommendation for a Reiki practitioner. Our hairdresser swore by her, which may sound random, but trust me, our hairdresser has really good energy. He's definitely not self-destructing with stress. And hair, as we all know, can be very challenging.

The Reiki practitioner, Patti, happened to have a cancellation right after my appointment with the pain doctor, so I went straight there. When I walked into her office, I was at rock bottom, but I would never let a stranger see how defeated I felt. I shook her hand and said, "Hi, nice to meet you" in that same little show voice that I used whenever I was nervous, the overpolite, apologetic little-girl voice that meant to say, *I'm not a diva, and I'm sorry in advance for . . . for being me, I guess.* And then, just to be clear, I apologized for being late.

The room was toasty warm. In a sweet voice she asked if there were any areas I needed addressed. I just said, "My head and my stomach," without elaborating. I got under the covers, lying first faceup, then later on my belly with my eyes closed. She moved her hands above me without touching my body, but I could sense where she was by the heat of her hands.

The session lasted about an hour. Afterward, when I sat up, the first thing she said was "Wow, you have a lot going on. You're about to go through a lot of changes, a whole reassessment of your life." Had the pain doctor called ahead to tell her exactly what he'd told me? Impossible—they didn't know about each other. But how could it be that they were saying the exact same thing?

I wasn't ready to trust this woman: we'd just met, and I'd been to a lot of different doctors and healers. I just said, "Okay, interesting."

Then she said, "I see pain in your head. Your head is busy all the time. You explain too much. You're always apologizing for everything, explaining yourself to others. What might seem quirky to everyone else is too busy for you. You need to calm down."

I said, "Okay." But what I was thinking was *I get it. I get it. I need to calm down. Everyone agrees. But easier said than done.*

She said, "You've given up your spirit. You've given up your self. When I was up by your throat, you started coughing and choking." I knew what she'd meant. I'd definitely had a weird response when I felt her hands near my throat. I chalked it up to fear of death by strangulation, but she had a better theory. "You've lost your voice completely in your life," she said.

I said, "Sometimes it's easier to push it down."

She said, "But you have a voice and you have feelings. If you don't speak them, you're repressing that." I was. Maybe that was the knot in my stomach.

She said that it was all pretty dark and heavy until she turned me over on my stomach. "A beaming star came out of your back. You have not reached your finest moment yet. Your shining star hasn't risen yet, but it will." I could see it now. The Oscar in my hand. The montage of magazines saying, "Turns Out Tori Can Act, After All." And "She's Actually Kind of Cute." And "Meryl Streep Passes the Torch to . . . Tori." I shook myself out of it. Patti went on.

"I saw your backbone grow. This year, if you allow yourself to grow, you'll grow a backbone." Wait a minute. Wasn't my tailbone too long already? If it grew anymore, I'd have a tail. And then I really would be a one-of-a-kind actress, but not for the right reasons.

But oh my God, that beaming star. Maybe the leaf that Mama Lola had glued to my tailbone had worked its magic. That Mama

Lola—she had me figured out. I was always looking for instant results, but I didn't have to change who I was overnight. I was going to grow. I could do it, little by little. Patti and I talked further, and I became more and more confident that I could help myself get better.

Patti said, "You'll start to change, and when you do, you'll see that everyone around you will change."

I said, "What happens when I start that change?"

She said, "Hope. Hope grows." Then she hugged me and left the room. I started crying. Hope. I had just met this woman and she had given me hope.

I believe in fate. I believe that things happen for a reason. I believe in hope. I believe in answers. And I believe in Christian Louboutin.

The pain doctor and the Reiki practitioner had told me the same thing. My illness was not going to be solved by any kind of medicine or treatment. Or not by those alone. If I wanted to get better, I had to make changes to my life. I was Dorothy in Oz: the way back home was in my hands the whole time.

I have tons of work lined up for next year. Making life changes would mean pushing that aside, taking time for myself, getting back to basics, back to me and back to my family. I wasn't going to stop working. But I needed to find a way to run six businesses without micromanaging. I needed to be able to clear my head. I needed to take a Saturday with my family. I needed to learn how

to manage all this—my work, my life, myself. I hadn't figured out
how exactly to do it yet, but I knew I had to rethink my life if I
was going to enjoy it. I made a pact with myself. I had to make
changes. I didn't know what they would be, but I knew I needed
a metamorphosis.

The next week, for the first time, I allowed Dean to take Stella
and Liam to school without me. We've always made sure filming stopped so I could be at Stella's Mommy & Me class. But
when I couldn't do it, she had to go with Dean. That should have
been fine, but I was so worried that people would see Stella in
the Mommy & Me class with him or our babysitter and think,
"Of course Tori Spelling doesn't bring her own kid." I didn't even
want them to see our babysitter dropping Liam off.

I missed two weeks of classes. When I went back to the school,
there was a new mother in the class. I went up to her and introduced myself. She was very friendly and we chatted the whole
time. But a few days later our babysitter, Paola, came to me and
Dean and told us that something had happened at school on a
day when she was there instead of me. All the moms were gathered for Circle Time, an opportunity for the parents to bring up
issues or questions they have concerning their kids. On the new
mom's second day at the school, she started talking about how
nannies shouldn't bring kids to school, only parents. According
to Paola, she said, "Obviously she doesn't value this class if she
doesn't come," then turned to Paola and said, "Don't take this

personally; it's not about you." The new mom said that she didn't know something like that would happen at this school and she suggested I was getting special treatment because I was a celebrity. The teachers were trying to settle her down, asking if she wanted her nanny to bring her child, which she did not. Finally they told her that it wasn't a matter for Circle Time and that she should take it up with the front office. Paola had been mortified, and now I was too. She had been so nice to my face.

This was exactly what I feared. I grew up being criticized for my looks, for my acting, for having a part on my daddy's show. I eventually got used to that. I'm under constant speculation for my weight and my marriage, which bugs me a little but I can stand it. The one criticism I can't abide is of my parenting.

Back at school the next day Dean and I talked to the teacher. I said, "This woman doesn't know me or my situation. I've been really sick. It wasn't because I was busy or didn't feel like coming or value the time."

The teacher said, "You don't need to explain yourself. It's not our policy that moms have to be here with the children. If you're sick or busy, whatever the reason, we still want the child to be able to come to school." I felt attacked, but the teacher said, "You should feel safe in this environment. You've been here for two years with both your children."

To make decisions based on fear of being judged isn't good parenting. I decided to take what people might think out of the equation. What was best for my children? Liam loved school. Stella would have a great time with or without me. If I was working or sick, it was better for her to be there with someone else. She loved it. It seemed like a simple decision, but it was hard for me.

A few days later one of the mothers came up to me and said, "I just want you to know that what happened in Circle Time was inappropriate and unacceptable."

I started to say, "I've been sick—" but she stopped me.

"You shouldn't have to defend yourself. It's not her business."

Another mom chimed in, "Don't worry, we have your back." That helped. The moms who knew me were on my side. But it was a harsh reminder that there are always people who want to assume the worst, and it made a hard decision harder.

I wanted to slow down, to take life in. I knew if I tried to change everything all at once, the results wouldn't be meaningful, so I tried to make other small changes. Dean and I decided that we'd start taking the kids on walks to the Coffee Bean. Just a simple walk in the neighborhood, a new family ritual.

Liam took to the idea right away. He started saying, "Go for coffee, go for coffee!" every morning. He loved our time together. So one morning when Dean was working, I took the kids by myself.

I rolled the double stroller into the Coffee Bean. It was a three-wheeled stroller with stadium seating, which meant that Liam was in front of and above Stella, who was in a little hideaway seat between the two rear wheels. I was in line to pick up my white chocolate soy latte and hot chocolates for the kids when I heard what sounded like a gunshot. There was a collective gasp.

I instinctively ducked; the other patrons dropped to the floor. Everyone froze. There was silence. Then, as everyone was sort of peeking out from under their arms to see what was going on, I looked down at the stroller. One of the tires was deflating, rapidly. It had burst. Everyone looked over at me.

I said, "Oh my God, it's our tire." I was embarrassed.

Then I realized that Stella was sitting right next to the tire when it burst. That deafening boom was right next to her ears. I knelt down to her and said, "That was loud."

Stella echoed me, "Loud!"

I said, "It was really loud!"

She said, "Really loud!"

I said, "Too loud!"

She said, "Too loud!" Oh my God, she was telling me that it was too loud. She was deaf.

I screamed, "Oh my God, her ears."

She said, "Ears." She was trying to tell me that her ears hurt! What else could I do? I pushed the crippled stroller out of Coffee Bean and immediately dialed the pediatrician.

I'm friendly with our pediatrician, and she knows how I can be. So when she came on the phone, I said, "I'm sorry to bother you, and I'm sure this is ridiculous, but you know my irrational fears. Anyway, our tire popped. It sounded like a gunshot and it was four inches from Stella's ear. I think she might be deaf. Is that possible?" The pediatrician was laughing. This was very funny to her.

She said, "Absolutely not. Stella is fine."

I said, "But it sounded like a gunshot! And when I asked her if it was loud, she said, 'Too loud.' "

The pediatrician managed to stop laughing long enough to say, "You could fire a gun next to her and she'd be fine."

I was making small changes, but my irrational fears were still there. I had no idea how to get rid of them. And I was supposed to fly to New York for a personal appearance the next week.

Why, Murray, Why?

I decided to pay another visit to Patti, the Reiki practitioner, to see if she could help me with my fear of flying. I went to her the day before Dean and I were due to fly to New York. It was going to be the first time that we had flown together, leaving both kids at home. I was convinced that we would orphan them.

At the end of the session, when Patti gave me her notes, she said, "It's odd. I saw John Hughes again." I had told her that when I was a teenager I used to listen to John Hughes soundtracks, that they made me happy. Now I explained that in *Say Anything*, Diane (played by Ione Skye) is afraid to fly. At the end of the movie she takes her first flight. Lloyd (John Cusack) tells her that you're safe on the flight when you hear the *ding* that means it's safe to turn on electronic devices. The movie ends with the *ding*. Ever since I saw *Say Anything*, I wait for the *ding*. Once I hear it, I feel a little better on the flight.

Now that we had my eighties movie inspirational sound track energies harnessed, Patti asked me to explain exactly what I was afraid of when I flew. I said I thought I feared the lack of control and that I also feared dying. I told her, "What if everyone on that flight is supposed to die? What if it's their time?"

Then she said, "Do you live every day this way? Believing the worst is going to happen?"

"Yes," I said. "All day long I create these what-if scenarios in my mind." Then I walked her through a day of the what-ifs: What if I step out into the street at the wrong time and a car hits me? What if someone is hiding in that elevator, waiting for me to get on all by myself so he can kill me? What if that scaffolding collapses just as I walk under it? What if I'm taken down by a falling brick and the tabloid headlines read, "Spelling Killed by Flying TrajecTORI"?

I was (half) joking, but Patti didn't laugh. She listened. And asked more questions. And then she told me that my fear of flying didn't have anything to do with flying. I gave her a "whatchyoutalkinbout" look. Of course I was afraid of flying. Hello? That was the whole point.

But she told me that all these tragic fantasies were symptoms of one bigger issue. I compulsively imagined a horrible ending because . . . wait for it . . . deep down I didn't think I deserved the happy ending. If I created the tragedy, then I wouldn't have to create my happy ending. Whoa. My mind was reeling. This was it—the first time in my life that I'd heard a real explanation for all the self-torture. Dean would be amazed. I had to call him. And Jenny. I had to text Mehran. But the session wasn't quite over.

She told me that my third eye was craving nuts and that maybe a nutty shake would be a tasty treat. Okay, now we were done.

She was right. I knew she was right. Not necessarily about the nutty shake, although that did sound delicious. She was right that I didn't believe in a happy ending. I couldn't see it. A tragic end was easier to imagine, because why would everything just turn out well? I didn't deserve a happy ending. I burst into tears.

When I'd calmed down a little, I looked at Patti and said, "What do I do? How am I supposed to change?"

She said, "Write your happy ending." Suddenly I understood Murray.

After my mother's Christmas party my friend Dana and I went to a bookstore on Ventura to pick up Christmas presents for Randy and Leah. I wanted to get Leah a book about baking since we'd talked about it at the party. For Randy I needed a travel book to go with the camera I'd already gotten him. I was in a rush, but when I saw some rescue dogs outside the store, I hesitated. Dana said, "Don't even look." We hurried into the store.

I found the books for Leah and my brother, but then I saw a beautiful book on sushi. I thought of how Randy and I used to go for sushi together so often. I wanted to get the book for him, but it didn't go with the camera. It would ruin the travel theme of his gift. So I left the store without it.

On Christmas Day we were going to have dinner with my mom, Randy, and Leah at the Polo Lounge. In the days leading up to the dinner I couldn't stop thinking about that sushi book. It just kept coming back into my head. So when we were in a paper store the day before to buy last-minute Christmas cards, I told Dean that I was going to duck into the bookstore next door to pick up the sushi book.

As I came out of the bookstore, Dean met up with me. I saw the same dog rescue group set up outside the store with a row of dogs in cages. I said, "Aw, can we just look at the dogs?"

As Dean and I peered at the dogs, the woman from the shelter said, "Are you looking for anything in particular?"

I said, "No, we have enough dogs. We're just looking." But something made me ask if this was all the dogs they had.

She said, "No, there are a few more. We're about to bring them out." We weren't about to get another dog, especially not on Christmas Eve, but for some reason we waited anyway. The woman brought out three more carriers. In one of them was a small, light brown, old-looking mutt. His face said, "Nobody loves me. Nobody cares." He was like the Eeyore of dogs.

Now, Dean is not into dogs. I mean, he likes them, but I'm the rescue fanatic. Dean looked at this sad old dog and said, "Who's this guy? What's his story?"

She said, "His name's Cane. He's really old, about ten years old. We don't have much hope for him getting adopted. He was found out on the street. He's never lived indoors." Dean asked to take Cane out. She brought him out of his cage and he just stood there. We walked him around a little bit. Dean picked him up and said, "I really like this guy." When Dean held him up close, I saw that they looked alike. It was something about their eyes.

Or their snouts. (Sorry, Dean.) Dean said, "It's Christmas Eve, should we take him home?"

I said, "Really?"

Dean said, "I feel bad for this little old fellow."

If Dean was in the mood to add dogs to our household, I was going to milk it for all it was worth. I said, "Great. How about this one too?" Dean thought one new unplanned dog was enough.

The shelter woman gave me a little Christmas hat for him. I put it on his head; we put his leash on and led him to the car. He was mellow. He just went with the flow.

On our way home I tweeted a picture of Cane, asking my followers for name suggestions. Someone suggested Murray. Dean and I looked at each other and said, "That's it!" He was Murray Cane McDermott.

Liam has never shown much interest in our dogs. But when we came in the front door and said, "Liam, Liam! Come meet your new dog!" he ran over and said, "My dog! That's my dog." Liam fed Murray treats. Murray nuzzled him. It was a match. Dean said, "Murray's the perfect dog. I'm going to get a sidecar for Murray. He'll wear a helmet and ride next to me when I bike." My policy was no children or dogs allowed on motorcycles, surprise, surprise, but I was in too good a mood to protest.

That night was Christmas Eve. Jenny and her family came over for dinner. I made stew (No shepherd's pie! Never again!) and Murray helped out by lying below, waiting for droppings. There were no presents under the tree yet—I was waiting for the kids to go to sleep—just a large white tree skirt made of shaggy faux fur.

Murray, who had never had a house to call his own, made his way over to the tree and lay down under it as if he'd been part of the family for years. Liam curled up next to him. A dog and his boy, side by side under the Christmas tree. It was a Norman Rockwell moment.

Christmas dinner was casual and nice. When I gave my brother the sushi book, I explained that it didn't go with the gift but it was so him that I had to get it. He looked at me and smiled. In that moment we connected and I knew I'd made the right decision.

The next morning—the day after Christmas—Liam came running up to us saying, "What's wrong with my dog?" We followed him into the kitchen to Murray's carrier, where he lay half in, half out. He raised his head slowly, with great effort. He was noticeably sick. Then he threw up.

Mehran stayed with the kids while Dean and I took Murray straight to the vet. The vet's staff said he had a high temperature but that the vet was still out for Christmas vacation so we should go to the emergency vet. We drove straight there. They did an ultrasound and found a mass in Murray's abdomen. I thought back to my cancer scare in Maui. Had Murray lived the best life he could? Had he taken life by the balls knowing that this day would one day come? I hoped that in spite of his hardscrabble life, Murray had enjoyed some prime bones in his youth.

The vet asked for permission to put him under so they could give him an X-ray and possibly surgery. She told us that she thought it might be cancer, and if it was, she had no idea how far it had spread. The rescue group had said he was probably ten, but she thought he was older. His chances weren't good. I told her to do whatever it took to save him. She wanted to know if I wanted her to try to resuscitate him. I said, "Yes, of course."

She said, "I've never seen it work."

I said, "On animals or on people?"

She said, "Either."

I said, "Do it. Please try."

The nurse carried Murray out to see us. I held out my hands to him. He put his chin in my hands, surrendering the weight of his head, and just looked at me. It was like he knew the prognosis and had already accepted his fate. I wanted to give him hope, but the nurse was looking at me, so I self-consciously whispered in his ear. I said, "Don't give up just because you found a home. Stay with us. There's more for you. A family."

Murray had five hours of surgery. When the vet called, she said, "He survived surgery. I can't believe this guy. He's a Christmas miracle. I never thought he'd make it." But half an hour later she called again to say that he'd gone into cardiac arrest. They had tried to resuscitate him, they had done everything possible, but now she wanted permission to pull the plug. I gave it. Two days after we rescued him, Murray was gone.

The vet said that in surgery they discovered that Murray had eaten one of those little plastic squares they use to close the plastic around loaves of bread. She said he'd eaten it about a week earlier. It had torn him up inside. His fate had already been sealed when we brought him home. That bread clip was already going to kill him.

We didn't say anything to Liam. He was only two and a half; we decided that was best. Two days later when he asked where Murray was, we said he was at the vet and that his sister was going to come live with us. Liam just said, "My Murray. My first dog."

Why had we picked this dog? Out of thirty dogs, why did we connect to the one who had twenty-four hours to live? Why Murray?

Now, in the treatment room with Patti, I understood. In life there are miracles and disappointments at every turn. Murray was both for us, and I wouldn't have done anything differently. Nothing. His old life was a mystery to me, but with us Murray had twenty-four hours of what he deserved. He had Christmas with a family and a boy. He wrote his own happy ending. If he could do it, I could.

My life was changing. I felt it. If she had told me six months ago to write my happy ending, I wouldn't have known where to begin, but now I was starting. Letting go of perfection. Making time for small moments with my family. Instead of making my fear of flying magically disappear, I would work on it. I would rewrite it. I would teach myself another way of being.

After using up an entire tissue box, I left Patti's office. I was starving. And I had a yeast infection. So I went to Gelson's supermarket. In Gelson's I wandered up and down the aisle looking for Monistat, which falls right between tampons and condoms on the scale of embarrassing supermarket purchases. As I searched, my internal fan radar started beeping. There was a girl on her cell phone who kept popping up. No matter which aisle I turned down, there she was. I was a mess from my crying jag, so not in the mood. I avoided eye contact. I found the feminine hygiene section, grabbed a box of Monistat, and went over to the hot food to find some lunch. Just as I was picking up a rotisserie chicken, I heard, "Hey, you're Tori, right?" I had the chicken in one hand and the Monistat in the other. I turned around, trying to subtly drop the Monistat out of view. The last thing I needed was to see the tabloid headline "Tori Is Yeasty, Buys Chicken." The box fell onto the hot food counter, faceup for all to see.

I said, "Yes, I'm Tori. Hi."

"Hi, I'm Miss Beverly Hills," she said. "Wow, you're much shorter in person. Do you want a picture of Miss Beverly Hills?"

I said, "Oh no, that's okay." Was she offering me a picture of herself? No, I didn't feel a desperate need for her headshot.

She said, "You won't take a picture with me?"

I said, "Oh, you mean with me in it? Sorry, not today, I'm looking really haggard." Haggard was the least of it. I'd just been crying for an hour. Didn't she realize that not only did I have no idea how to write my own happy ending but I was also feeling yeasty? I kept trying to push the Monistat out of view on the hot food buffet, but Miss Beverly Hills was otherwise occupied.

She said, "Here, I can take a quick picture. If you don't like it, we can delete it. Wow, you really are short!"

I said, "I'm five feet five."

She said, "Well, I'm six feet so everyone looks short to me." She held her phone in front of us and took a snapshot. She examined it, then passed it to me for my approval. In the picture my face was a peanut on her boob. I was tiny, makeup-free, and wan. She said, "Is the picture okay?"

I said, "Yes, it's fine."

She said, "Okay, well, I'll probably see you at the gym. Bye." I watched her go, thinking, *What are you talking about? I never go to the gym.*

The next day Dean, my agent Gueran, and I boarded our flight for New York. Every single time I ever fly, when I'm entering the plane I put my right foot over the threshold first. Then I glance at the outside of the plane, checking to see if there's any last sign that I should not get on the flight. I cross onto the plane and look to the left, into the cockpit, trying to make eye contact with the pilots. I always pause, hoping that a pilot will turn around, see the fear on my face, take pity on me, and bring me into the cockpit. Meeting the pilots and sitting in the cockpit seemed like it might give me confidence in their abilities and quell my fears. I've been flying since I was eighteen, and not once has either pilot ever turned around and talked to me.

So I went through my plane entrance ritual, then Dean, Gueran, and I went to our seats. A male flight attendant came over. He said, "Hi, Tori, how are you? Can I take your coat?" I was wearing a big teddy bear coat, vintage Gucci. As he took it, I saw him look at the label, smile, and walk away. I thought, *Oh good, he's one of mine.* Maybe he was even the same flight attendant who had announced, "Welcome to Los Angeles, birthplace and residence of Tori Spelling." The flight was already looking up.

Patti had inspired me to try to make this flight different. Wanting to reassure myself, I walked up to the front of the plane and in my little, apologetic voice I said to the friendly flight attendant, "I'm a really scared flyer. I just wanted to know if there's going to be any turbulence."

He said, "Oh, you're scared? Would you like to come talk to the pilots? Would that make you feel better?" No way this was happening.

I said, "I've always wanted to talk to the pilots!"

He brought me to the cockpit. The pilots turned around when we came in, and my flight attendant friend said, "Hi, I have Tori Spelling here. She's a nervous flyer. Can she talk to you for a few minutes?" He opened up the jump seat for me and I sat down.

The pilots said, "So tell us, why are you scared of flying?"

I wasn't about to explain the whole thing. My dad's phobia. My what-ifs. My need to write my own happy ending. Instead, in my little voice, I said, "I don't know. I've always been scared. Everything makes me nervous."

Then I said, "I've always wanted to be asked to sit in the cockpit. I've been flying for almost twenty years and I've never had the chance."

The copilot said, "Pretty girl like you? I can't believe that." Was the copilot flirting with me? We made conversation. They talked about the flight a little. The copilot was definitely flirting with me! He was so attentive that I started wondering if my hair looked good. I wasn't dressed for flirting! Now I wasn't nervous, just ready to go back to my seat, but they were still chatting away. Didn't they have a plane to fly? They were so chill.

Finally another flight attendant came in and said, "We're ready to go." There was a plane full of people, all in their seats waiting.

I didn't know how to say good-bye. Should I shake hands? Salute? At a loss, I said, "See you on the ground safely!" and gave them a "way to go, fellas" air punch. So dorky. They turned to their instruments and I stood up to go. I wasn't even fully turned around when the copilot turned his head to check out my ass. Yes he did!

Back at my seat I told Gueran that the copilot had looked at my ass. I said, "Doesn't it look flat in these leggings?"

He said, "No, it looks good." Okay, then. Everything was working in my favor. This flight was really coming together. *Ding.*

It was the first flight in my life that I didn't shed a single tear. It really happened. I changed. Not completely—I was still nervous. But it was odd. I was nervous in a way that was kind of familiar and not unpleasant, like the way I might be nervous at the dentist about having a cavity. I just kept saying to myself, "Stop fantasizing about tragedy. Start writing your happy ending." Something had changed. Something in my core being wasn't nervous. My heart wasn't pounding the way it usually did. The butterflies weren't butterfly army training in my belly. There was some inner calm. When we had turbulence, the bumps made me go back to negative thoughts, but even then I'd just start talking myself to the happy place again. I pictured myself at Liam's wedding. In the visual I kept seeing him wearing a bow tie, which wasn't my ideal, but I could get past it. It was his wedding, after all.

I couldn't make that decision for him, though I could certainly make a recommendation. Then I pictured Liam getting married on that plane. It wasn't an ideal party location—I don't see him having a theme wedding—but I could work with it. The table numbers would be displayed on airsick bags. The servers could wear flight wings. Yeah, that could be fun.

One morning a couple of weeks ago I stirred and opened my eyes to find Dean lying on his side, propped on an elbow, staring at me. I immediately panicked. Was I drooling? Had I been snoring like a beast again? Were there crusty sleep boogers caked in my eyes? I said, "What's wrong?"

Dean smiled. He said, "Here's me. Here's you. I love you." It was the same thing he'd said to me at a little bar in Ottawa when we first met and fell in love.

Still trying to rub nonexistent eye boogers away, I looked at him and said simply, "I love you too." It was one of those moments of reconnection, where a look or a sentence or both put everything back into perspective. In that moment I had never felt more in love with my husband.

Our lives kept changing. We had babies and work, hobbies and sickness, new and unexpected demands on our time. But at the heart of it all there was *us*. Tori and Dean. Dean and Tori. Good and bad, up and down, we were in it together. We had each other, always, to propel ourselves forward and to fall back on.

Even though I'd only had six hours of sleep and knew that the kids would wake soon, suddenly sleep didn't matter. All I wanted to do was make love to my husband. Liam and Stella must have gotten the memo because for the first time ever they both slept past eight a.m. So Dean and I behaved like two teens in love and made crazy love, cuddled, laughed, and talked. We talked, and we heard each other. It was an amazing morning in the McDermott household.

Dean still races motorcycles, but I know that his number one hobby is his wife and kids. I try not to nag or to communicate with Dean through our two-year-old son (although that was kind of fun). We realize how lucky we are to have each other. I love Dean more every day, every year that passes. He has given me the life and love and family that I always dreamed of as a little girl. There will be more ebbs and flows. That's how a marriage evolves. But for now we are just loving each other as best we can.

Afterword

Not long after we got home from New York, I had a sweet moment with Liam. Stella was taking her nap. Liam and I were in his room. He was sitting in my lap with books fanned out around him on the floor. For some reason he was going through the dogs' names. He said, "I like my dogs. I like Ferris. I like Chiquita." Then he laid his head back in my lap, looked up at me, and said, "I like you."

I said, "I like you too."

Then he said, "You're my mommy." We'd never had a conversation like this, where he took a moment to see and love our relationship.

I said, "You're my baby."

He sat up straight, turned to me, and said, "I am not a baby." Then, in a more modest, matter-of-fact tone, he said, "I'm just Superman."

I said, "Well, you'll always be my baby."

But he said, "No, Mama, Stella's your baby."

I said, "Okay."

Then he said, "Read, Mama, read." I started reading a book called *Fuzzy Land.* Liam knew the words to the book by heart. He said them aloud as I read. So I sat there reading the story, hoping he couldn't hear me crying. Then my tears started dripping onto his hair and I hoped he couldn't feel me crying. He wasn't my baby anymore. It had happened so quickly. He wasn't even three years old. If he could grow so much, learn so much, and change so much in so little time, then so could I. I was doing it for him, for Stella, for Dean, and for myself.

And so my quest goes on. Balance still eludes me. I haven't found the magic key that will unlock my health problems, and sometimes I think I'm so out of whack that it's hopeless. But I'm determined to search. I'm open to answers. I have hope.

I've found work that I love, and with it came a new stability. Dean and I have a home and a family together. To the outside eye it looks like my life is in place. But I feel something life-changing on the horizon. Sometimes I fantasize about moving to a little house in the country where I can live a simple life and be that girl who ran away to her parents' laundry room. Dean's on board for that, so long as there's a dirt bike track. Dean's always on board.

I love what I already have—my children, my husband, my friends, my work, my mother and brother, the life that I always dreamed of, and my ambitions for our future together. No matter how overwhelming it is, I still see the joy and promise of that life. I'm still living it, and I'll continue to fight for it. That's what balance is about, right? Tightrope walkers may appear to walk effortlessly across a line, but they are working with all their muscles, with all their being, to fight the forces that constantly pull them in different directions. The more you train those muscles, the easier it is to walk that fine line. And so I creep forward, wobbly and fearful, but committed to all that I have and all that I am.

Acknowledgments

I'd like to thank all the people in my life who have been a part of my amazing, fun, emotional, zany, humorous, insightful, and rewarding journey so far and still choose to stick around as together we enter uncharted terriTORI . . .

Dean . . . My soul mate. We've been through a lot in a short time and continue to prove that true love conquers all. You are my one true love and have given me the life and family I only thought I'd ever find in my dreams. You MADE my reality.

Liam . . . My sweet gentle soul. My beautiful baby boy. My Monkey. Keep entertaining. Mommy loves you, Super Dude.

Stella . . . My angelic girly girl. My Buggy. You have mama's fire and love of purses and shoes. I love your heart and soul. I love you.

Jack . . . It's been a pleasure watching you grow from a little boy into a bright, confident young man. I love you.

Mom . . . I've always loved you and always will. We know our truth. Family is everything.

Randy . . . I love you, Genie. I am so proud of the man you've become and the life you have created for yourself.

Mehran . . . You are the greatest UN-love of my life. You love me unconditionally and never cease to have patience for my crazy brain. You believe in me even when I forget to believe in myself. You are my chic rock. Truly my best friend and my gay husband forever.

Jenny . . . My best friend and sister. You've exemplified the meaning of "old friends are the best friends." You inspire me daily and give me strength when I sometimes feel like I have none. I love you.

Scout and Bill (aka The Guncles) . . . You have given my family love beyond love. Before I can ask, you know and are there. You make me laugh and nurture me when I need to cry. You've shown me that family is there for you no matter what.

Amy, Sara, Jennifer, Marcel, James . . . Friends come and go BUT true friends are forever. Thank you for your patience and love over the past year and never giving up on me.

Patsy . . . Fate brought our lives together, but love made us family. You have shown me unconditional love and have taught me the value of family. You mean the world to us. Always.

Dale . . . Although we are far apart I know you are always there for me, Big Sis! Thanks for reminding me that family always has your back and gives unconditional love.

Aunt Kay . . . For your continued love for our family. And your amazing generosity. You spoil the kids and we love it!

My Canadian family . . . We don't see each other or speak often enough but you are all always in my heart.

Brandy . . . For listening to me through it all and being a true girlfriend. Plus, you always make me look beautiful when sometimes I don't feel it.

Ruthanne . . . My personal crusader! Without your belief in me I wouldn't be where I am today professionally and emotionally. You go beyond the call of duty as my agent and you then go beyond that as my friend. You've made me believe that Tori Spelling can make it happen because you are right there by my side.

Gueran . . . You constantly inspire me to be more than I ever thought possible for myself. You've helped build this dream. Where some talk, you make happen. My books happened because you believed in me. Thank you for that gift of confidence and for being so damn good at what you do. You are my friend and my family.

Jacob . . . For believing in me and being a good friend through it all. We've come a long way and did it together. You were loyal to me, and I'll always be loyal to you. And for giving me one hell of an opening story in this book!

Jamie . . . My strength! Making me always feel I'm worth it. And then getting it for me.

Meghan and Jill . . . The press builds us up to knock us down and you are both there to catch me. Your personal investment in my family is amazing. I always feel safe with you and loved. Thank you for always going to bat for me.

Randy and Fenton . . . My partners and friends. We've created a wonderful life and business together. I'm WOWED by how lucky I am to have you and your constant support. You make me dream Bigger.

Our *T&D* family/crew . . . What started as a business turned into the family we've created. I don't believe in coincidences. And I know each and every one of you is meant to be with me on this journey. You've all been loyal to no end and I love you and deeply value our relationships.

Oxygen . . . Thank you for giving our family a second home! For continuing to believe in me, my dreams, and all my business ventures.

Megan . . . Story brought us together but fate brought our lives so much more. You have been my strength this past year when I sometimes felt I had none. You know how much you mean to me. Thank you for sharing, being, and growing with me.

Gary and Eleanor . . . For always trusting my goals. For supporting me and believing I'll attain them.

Patrick Price . . . My Editorial Husband. Without you this process wouldn't be as fun or seamless. Thanks for getting me. You are my written ROCK.

Jen Bergstrom . . . Thank you for finding my voice smart and humorous. You make me believe that wit and candor can achieve anything.

Jen Robinson . . . Thank you for going to bat for my books and making people take notice.

Michael Nagin . . . For your vision and charm and letting my type A personality micromanage details.

Mike Rosenthal . . . For always understanding I have my side, angle, and pose and for taking unbelievably beautiful pictures. We make good covers!

Gallery Books/Simon & Schuster . . . For continuing to give my voice a home base. You believe in me and I look forward to creating more bestsellers together!

Hilary . . . My visionary partner in the written word. For always getting me, being the voice of reason, and sometime therapist. Let's write our happy ending.

Dan Strone . . . Three books later! Thanks for being instrumental in making it happen.

Patti Penn . . . For giving me hope. And making me believe in me again.

Dr. Graff-Radford . . . For not taking my bullshit and for not giving up on me.

Dr. Wexler . . . For knowing my truth and always helping me to get back to it.

Dana . . . For being my health/emotional wingman. I deeply thank you. You ARE nurturing!

Derick . . . For loving my family and being the constant optimist. Your positive energy is infectious.

Isabel . . . For always looking out for me and my family. For loving us and knowing me so well. You have been my constant through all these years. And for loving the doggies so much.

Paola . . . You inspire me as a mom and as a woman. Your work ethic is tireless and your love for our kids is undeniable. We are blessed to have you as part of our family.

Coco and Susana . . . Thank you for your love, care, and loyalty.

Cheyenne . . . You are such a positive in my life and was always there to listen when I couldn't find answers. Thank you.

My dog babies . . . I may have rescued each of you, but you've rescued me in so many ways. I love you. And thank you, Much Love Animal Rescue (muchlove.org), for giving my animal rescue work a home.

My Twitter followers . . . For always believing in me and supporting me and for giving me a family to reach out to day or night.

Love, Tori xoxo